GOD'S
HOSTAGE

GOD'S HOSTAGE

A TRUE STORY OF PERSECUTION, IMPRISONMENT, AND PERSEVERANCE

ANDREW BRUNSON
WITH CRAIG BORLASE

Authentic

© 2019 by Andrew Brunson
25 24 23 22 21 20 19   7 6 5 4 3 2 1

Published in 2019 by Authentic Media Limited
PO Box 6326, Bletchley, Milton Keynes, MK1 9GG.
www.authenticmedia.co.uk

Published in the US by Baker Books a division of Baker Publishing Group
PO Box 6287, Grand Rapids, MI 49516-6287
www.bakerbooks.com

British Library Cataloguing in Publication Data
A catalogue record for this book is available from the British Library.

ISBN: 978-1-78893-127-4
978-1-78893-128-1 (e-book)

Printed and bound by CPI Group (UK) Ltd, Croydon, CR0 4YY

To our beautiful children—
Jordan, Jacqueline and Kevin, and Blaise

And to our Christian brothers and sisters in Turkey—
The prayer I prayed often for myself and over my family
while in prison
I now pray for you as well:

*Father God, pour out on your sons and daughters the courage,
the strength, the confidence, the perseverance, the endurance, and
the steadfastness of Jesus, that we may run the race set before
us and finish well, purified in the fires of faithful obedience,
tested and found worthy of Jesus, the King of Glory.*

CONTENTS

PART FOUR

PART FIVE

PART SIX

PART SEVEN

ACKNOWLEDGMENTS

THIS IS INEVITABLY AN INCOMPLETE LIST. Norine and I have not included everyone we want to thank, and beyond this, there are many who did things we are not even aware of. Throughout this process we have come to see that God has many of his people in places of influence and that he has many who know those in places of influence.

SO MANY IN THE WHITE HOUSE and the State Department did so much for us. Our thanks to the consular staff in Turkey for their faithful visits (and magazines!)—Norman Pflanz, Aroosha Rana, and especially Martin Thomen.

Chargé d'Affaires Phil Kosnett and his staff in Ankara went above and beyond for me and, along with his wife, Alison, provided support to Norine. Norine was released shortly after Phil met with the Turkish deputy prime minister. Jeffrey Hovenier was focused and engaged from the minute he took over as chargé d'affaires.

Assistant Secretary of State Wess Mitchell fought hard for us, and Ambassador Sam Brownback came to my trial and advocated for me.

We are grateful for Secretary of State Mike Pompeo's interest and commitment to action on our behalf, and to Vice President Mike Pence for being "on to this" from early on and giving such personal attention throughout.

President Donald Trump intervened for me again and again, taking unprecedented steps to secure my release.

WE ARE DEEPLY GRATEFUL to the many senators and members of the House of Representatives who monitored my situation and signed letters to the Turkish government requesting my release. In a time of sharp political division this was truly a bipartisan effort.

Senator Bob Corker was the first to raise my case to the highest levels of the Turkish government, and he organized a letter to President Erdogan from the Senate and then a second one from the Senate and House.

We were told that Senator James Lankford was "our hero on the Hill." Early on he met with the Turkish minister of justice, brought media attention to my plight, and throughout my imprisonment never stopped looking for ways to bring me home.

Senator Thom Tillis was tenacious. He visited me in prison, attended my first trial session, and made many speeches on the Senate floor that kept my name before his colleagues.

Senator Jeanne Shaheen was also committed to getting me out. Together with Senators Lankford and Tillis she introduced a bill to block the delivery to Turkey of the F-35 fighter planes in relation to my detention. Along with Senator Lindsey Graham she met with President Erdogan and then visited me in prison.

We are grateful to the office staff of these senators.

THE UNITED STATES COMMISSION on International Religious Freedom took up my case. Commissioners Sandy Jolley and Kristina Arriaga visited me in prison, Kristina returned for one of my court sessions, and Tony Perkins was at my last hearing and escorted us back to the US.

Our deep thanks to Erik Bethel at the World Bank.

Help also came from other governments, including Hungary, Israel, Canada, Monaco, Mauritania, and Sudan. In the European Parliament, ninety-eight MEPs from twenty-one countries wrote to President Erdogan urging him to release me.

THE AMERICAN CENTER for Law and Justice, Jay Sekulow, and our US attorney CeCe Heil in particular, were relentless in fighting for us. CeCe was truly available for us 24/7.

Middle East Concern, especially through Rob D., advocated and raised prayer for us in countries outside the US and provided much personal encouragement. Other advocacy groups and individuals also took on the challenge, including Rights & Resolution Advocates, Mark Siljander, Mark Finlay, Michael Bradle, Isaac Six, and Mark Burnett and Roma Downey. My good friend Dan Slade, coordinator of Partners in Harvest, did many things behind the scenes. Jeff Jeremiah, coordinator for the Evangelical Presbyterian Church, worked tirelessly on our behalf. Someone described him as latching on and not letting go. Norine's younger brother spent an enormous amount of time in the fight for me.

There are some who asked not to be named. You know who you are. Thank you.

HOW CAN WE THANK our worldwide family of believers? Protestants, Catholics, and Orthodox on every continent prayed, fasted, wrote letters, and prayed some more—some even facing persecution themselves. It was through their prayers that all the pieces moved for my release. A special thanks to children and teenagers who prayed and fasted, giving up meals, sweets, and electronics! We thank sunny Jayne for walking through this trial with Norine. The support from our brothers and sisters in Turkey who stood with us was especially meaningful. We were not alone.

PART ONE

1 | TIME TO COME HOME

I WAS SHAVING WHEN ALL OF THIS STARTED. Just standing in front of the fogged-up bathroom mirror in our apartment, barely noticing the typical sounds of hustle and bustle and traffic that drifted up from the narrow streets below. The city and I were both getting ready for an ordinary day that lay ahead.

That's when it hit me.

A thought, from out of the blue.

It's time to come home.

It startled me, and I jerked to a stop. I warily hit rewind in my mind. What had I just heard? It made no sense. I'm an American, but the day I stood in front of that bathroom mirror I did not think of the US as my home. Turkey was home. When we had bought this condo two years earlier, we knew that our knees could handle climbing to the fourth floor with no elevator, but we wondered if we would still be able to do it twenty years later. We were here for life.

It's time to come home.

My heart started to beat faster, because suddenly I feared that I knew what these words meant. I did not even want to think about the implications. I was home already. But my faith tells me that there is another home where I'm ultimately going. Could God be telling me it was time for me to die—time to come home to heaven?

It's time to come home.

I rebuked the thought. This can't be God. There are so many things left to do. No—it can't be time for me to die . . .

FOR TWENTY-THREE YEARS Norine and I had been living and working in Turkey.

We had met in the library at Wheaton College. Norine was there to study, while I was there looking for girls who were studying! I was determined to marry only someone who was willing to be a missionary. From the time I was a child I had a strong sense of call to missions that went all the way back to Hudson Taylor, the great missionary to China. When he was an old man, a mother took her two young sons to him and asked that he pray and set them aside for missions. They did become missionaries, and when one of them, Stanley Soltau, was an old man, my mother took me and my sister to him. She asked that he do for us what Hudson Taylor had done for him, and so he did. Because I was acting up I got a spanking, which marked the day for me. I was three years old, and I never forgot. I'm sure God put something in me that day that eventually took me to Turkey with Norine.

We arrived to Istanbul in 1993 and eventually settled in Izmir. We had started churches, hosted national conferences, set up a house of prayer, and invited people from other countries to come and join us in spreading the gospel to cities where not a single person had ever met a Christian. We already had a good-sized international team and were excited about a group of new missionaries who had arrived a few months before to do a year-long training program with us.

In our hometown of Izmir—ancient Smyrna, set on the Aegean Sea—we had worked with hundreds of refugees from Syria and Iraq who had fled from Assad and ISIS. Some had just been passing through, hoping to make the dangerous journey by boat to Europe. Others had stayed. A few had even decided to return to their own homeland, and for all of them we did what we could to help by providing blankets, heaters, food, milk for babies, and other items as donations from churches came in.

We had given our lives to this country where so much of Bible history took place. Now there are only around six thousand Muslim-background Christians out of a total population of more than eighty million. How do you start a church when only one out of every sixteen thousand Turks becomes a Christian? Sometimes it is very discouraging. When we arrived in 1993, twenty of us started a language course together. Four years later only five of us were still in the country. Eventually Norine and I were the only ones left from that group.

Our years in Turkey hadn't been easy. We knew of a few Christians who had been martyred for their work. We had received death threats. After the first ones, for a time I only wore tennis shoes and tied them tightly—something I rarely do because I like my shoes to fit loosely. Norine noticed and asked why I wasn't wearing sandals in the hot weather. My answer was simple and pragmatic: "Because I may need to run away."

That had been a scary time, especially for us as parents of young children, but it forced us to confront the issue of risk. Were we going to run at the first threat? How easy it then would be to get rid of us. We decided that we would stay until God showed us clearly to leave.

Recently we had spent time working among refugees on the Syrian border near a war zone, close enough for us to hear guns firing and bombs going off as the Kurds fought ISIS while we wondered if some fanatic would decide to kidnap us and hold us hostage. Norine was relieved every time she could return to Izmir after those trips. Overall, we had counted the cost. We knew the risks and we accepted them. Turkey was right where we needed to be. No, it couldn't be time to "come home."

I FINISHED SHAVING, got dressed, and took the short walk to our church. We had learned over the years that when people are seeking spiritually they often look for places where they know Christians will gather. That's why we put up a sign with a cross outside Resurrection Church, making it hard to miss. We were breaking no laws and never attempted to hide what we were doing. In fact, we wanted to be as visible as possible.

We had hesitated to rent this small building when we started the church. It was about all we could afford in the city center, but it was in the transvestite red-light district—would anyone come? Soon, however, we discovered it was a great location, with thousands of people walking by every day on their way to the sea and to busy pedestrian streets packed with shops and restaurants.

At some point we started stocking the two windowsills with Christian books and left a sign telling people they could help themselves. And they did. Soon we were giving away over one thousand New Testaments each month.

We never had a dull day in Turkey. Anything could happen on a Sunday—good or bad. We could pray for a visitor and see them healed or we could have someone yelling threats disrupt our meeting. When our door was open, some would venture in just to see a church for the first time. Many came with questions and almost all would accept prayer. Those who became Christians would often drop off after a few weeks or months as the pressure of family and friends got to them.

Another challenge was that all kinds of people came—from sincere seekers to those looking for gain or wanting to cause trouble. Over time people's motives would become clearer. We knew that secret police were in and out, and some people told us to be careful, but we had nothing to hide. With all this, it was amazing that the church grew at all.

As introverts, Norine and I were not a good fit for this very social culture, but God had tied our hearts to the people living in Turkey. And besides, we were convinced that God had given us and the church a very specific assignment—to prepare for a spiritual harvest.

I NEEDED TO FOCUS. There were classes to prepare. What I did not need was for that thought to come back. But it did. A soft whisper, but insistent.

It's time to come home.

I had rejected the thought earlier, but I could not shake the sense that this was God telling me to prepare to meet him—to die.

It wasn't the first time I'd stood in this church and thought that my life might be about to end.

Five and a half years earlier—on April Fool's Day—I'd stepped outside the church during a prayer meeting. It was typically busy in the street, and I was talking with a member of the church. A few of the transvestites were leaning out of the windows above us, smiling and waving at passersby just like they always did.

Suddenly, a man in a camouflage jacket caught our attention. He stood out for one simple reason. He was pointing a pistol at me from about twelve feet away. He was quiet but looked utterly determined, and his eyes were bright with rage. I froze. All I could focus on was the pistol that was trembling in his grip.

Six shots rang out in quick succession. Then he dropped the gun, reached into a bag on the ground beside him and pulled out a shotgun. My brain finally started working. As he struggled to close the gun, I knew he could not miss with a shotgun. And if he went into the church after he got me . . . it could be a massacre. I rushed over to the gunman and wrapped my arms around him from behind in a bear hug. He was bigger than me, stronger too. I held on desperately. As we struggled, he pulled the trigger and the shotgun went off. The gunman started screaming, "You started a church and we will not permit this! We will bomb you. We will kill you. You will give an account."

I felt nothing. I was numb. All I knew was that my life—and the lives of others—depended on not letting go.

Finally the police arrived and put the gunman down on the ground. Once they had taken him away, I walked back into the church. Adrenaline had helped me hang on to my would-be killer, but when I sat down the shock hit like a hurricane. My body started shaking and I could do nothing to stop it. As the tension bled off I was surprised that I was not afraid. God had spoken so many words about my future that I was confident that he still had plans for me in Turkey and would keep me alive until they were completed. So when the government assigned two police officers to me as bodyguards, I turned them down after a couple of weeks. I was sure I did not need them.

In the days and weeks that followed the attack, people asked us whether we would remain in Turkey. Norine and I knew the answer immediately. We had worked through this before: until God told us it was time to leave, we would stay.

As I stood alone in the church that October morning, I was no longer so confident that I *could* stay in Turkey. All those words about my future—was it possible that God was cutting short his plans for me?

It's time to come home.

"God," I prayed soberly. "There are so many things I have looked forward to. I don't want to leave my family. I am not ready. But I belong to you. You can do as you want. If you want me to come home to you, then prepare my heart."

THE NEXT DAY I went to meet Norine at a retreat center where she had spent the night to have some time alone in prayer. Together we drove out to the summer cottage that my parents had bought along the coast years ago. It had been a busy time for us, and though many of our friends had used the cottage, we hadn't spent nearly as much time there as we would have liked to. So it was good to be alone together and to finally try my new wetsuit and swim in the cool, clear waters of the Aegean Sea. We were happy. We had a lot to look forward to. Life was good.

I did not bring up the whole *It's time to come home* thought. It had flashed in my mind a couple more times that day, but I did not want to alarm Norine.

The following morning my phone rang, interrupting our lazy breakfast. It was a call from the church.

"Andrew? The police have just been here looking for you. They want to know when you're going to be around."

"Thanks," I said. "I'll be back in Izmir tomorrow."

Norine and I traded smiles.

"That could be good news," Norine said when I'd hung up. I agreed.

Months earlier we had applied for permanent resident status, which would allow us to live in Turkey until 2099—the rest of our lives. After hours of form filling, interviews at the local police station, and a lot of waiting, we were hopeful that the visas were ready. To both our minds, if the police wanted to see us it had to be about the residency application.

We had planned to spend a couple of days at the beach, but this was a good enough reason to cut it short. We busied ourselves cleaning the cottage and shutting it down for winter, loaded the van with food emptied from the cupboards along with our dripping wetsuits and towels, and made the drive back to Izmir.

It was dark by the time we pulled up in the street outside and made our way up the steps to our apartment.

"Look at this, my love," said Norine as she reached the front door and pulled off a piece of paper that had been taped to it. It was from the police, informing us that we were required to report to the local station as soon as possible.

I smiled. *Time to come home?* No, surely not yet.

2 | THE ARREST

I LOOKED AROUND AT THE APARTMENT as I waited for someone at the police station to pick up the phone. It was a real mess. We had arrived home too late the night before to deal with any of the things we'd brought back from the cottage. But I wanted to get this police visit out of the way before Norine started a day of cleaning and getting ready for guests.

"Yes?" It was 9:30 a.m., and the officer on the phone sounded bored already.

"Hello. My name is Andrew Brunson. I have a note saying that you need me and my wife to come to the station. Can we come by in an hour or two?"

"Yes."

"Okay. And what do we need to bring? Our passports?"

"Sure."

AFTER RETURNING from a morning workout, we prepared breakfast and ate together on the balcony—Norine her usual mixture of fruit and nuts, and for me eggs and beans.

It was October 7, the birthday of our oldest son, Jordan. Today he turned twenty-one—a milestone. Like all three of our kids, Jordan had grown up with us in Turkey. After he finished high school he returned to the States for college and was now a junior studying at Cornell University.

Our daughter, Jacqueline, was a student at the University of North Carolina, living in Chapel Hill. A couple months before, her boyfriend, Kevin, a US Army helicopter pilot, had asked us for her hand in marriage. He had just sent us a picture of the engagement ring, but it was to be a surprise—Jacqueline did not know about it yet.

Our youngest, Blaise, was in high school in North Carolina, living with my parents, struggling with a new home and culture away from us. On birthdays we especially felt the physical distance from our children. This was one of the costs of serving in Turkey.

NORINE AND I made the ten-minute walk down familiar streets to the station. We were sent to an upstairs room where an officer took our passports. He said nothing and stared at his computer screen like it was broken.

"Twenty-one years," mused Norine. "How did it go by so fast? We can call Jordan in a few hours—it's still too early in the States."

Eventually the officer shifted in his seat and turned to look at us both. "It says here," he said, pointing at the screen at the same time as he got to his feet, "that there's an order to deport you both. Follow me."

"What? On what basis?" The questions flew out of our mouths as we walked behind the officer back down the narrow stairway to the front desk. "There must be a mistake!"

The officer said nothing, but the station chief looked up at us between phone calls. "There is a deportation order for you. Sit down. Don't leave this room. We're keeping you here for a while."

So we sat where we were told to sit and did what we were told to do, which was to wait. We waited in the crowded office while he talked on the phone, cupping his hand over the mouthpiece in a way that made it hard for us to hear what he was saying. We waited while a sense of shock grew within us.

This could not be. Surely twenty-three years in Turkey would not end like this. We loved our church, a new training program had just started, the work with refugees was growing. Of course we knew that something like this *could* happen—but the timing . . . We had come today expecting permission to live here for the rest of our lives. We were stunned.

The chief called us over: "The order says G-82—Threat to National Security." I'd heard of G-82 before. It was a catchall that had been used to deport other missionaries.

Norine's smile was long gone, and I could feel that the blood had drained from my cheeks. I leaned close and kept my voice low. "Is it Eyup's doing?" Eyup was a troublemaker. After we asked him to leave our church a few months ago he had repeatedly threatened to accuse us of supporting the PKK, a Kurdish terrorist group. There was nothing to his accusation, of course, but could he be the one behind this?

"I don't know, but we need to make some calls."

THE FIRST NUMBER I dialed was the US Embassy in Ankara. I explained what little we knew, and they immediately put us in touch with a consular official.

Not all missionaries get ejected from Turkey the same way. A month earlier, one of our friends had been flying back to Turkey when he was told at the airport in Istanbul that his visa had been revoked and he would not be allowed to enter. We knew of others who had been called into the police station and told they had fifteen days to leave the country. From time to time people had been taken to deportation centers and from there escorted to the airport, but that was mainly for refugees.

The way I saw it, we needed to make sure that we could have the full fifteen days before leaving. During that time we could start an appeal and at the very least get our affairs in order. We needed a lawyer for this. I didn't think it would make much of a difference, but we had to try.

We must have spent the best part of an hour sitting there, huddling together as we scrolled through our contacts, making calls and then reporting to each other about them. Getting a prayer chain started was just as important as finding a lawyer—more so, in fact. As news about our plight spread in the Christian community, a few friends started arriving at the police station. After trying to get more information out of the police, they just waited with us.

WHILE I SAT THERE something clicked in my mind: the phrase *It's time to come home*. I wondered if God had given me this thought to prepare me for the shock of deportation, of losing our ministry in Turkey. He wanted to reassure me that this was in no way a surprise to him, and even more, that he was in it. I did not feel happy, I did not feel peace. But, in the midst of my racing emotions, confusion, and the loss of control, there was a glimmer of encouragement that God was actually involved.

A NUMBER OF POLICE OFFICERS were milling about us. The phone rang constantly and the volume of conversation increased. It felt like a lot of the activity was connected to us. The station chief had been on the phone as much as we had. As he ended a call, Norine approached and asked him whether we might be able to have the full fifteen days before we left.

He shrugged. "Well," he said, his hands open in front of him, "you haven't broken any laws here, so that should be possible. But it's not up to us. We're waiting for someone to make a decision."

His phone then rang. He turned away from us to answer it.

Norine returned to the seat beside me. We sat in silence.

"An order has come down," he said even before he'd replaced the receiver. "We're placing you under arrest."

THERE ARE TWO TYPES of arrest in Turkey—administrative, where the police hold you for another department that wants to see you; and judicial, where you're suspected to be guilty of a crime. The police chief told us that ours was administrative, and that we were being arrested on behalf of Migration Management, the department that handled deportations. It made some sense that they might choose to arrest us if they were deporting us, but it was hardly necessary. We weren't desperados—

they could tell us to leave, and we would. Hearing the chief's words—and noticing the change in his demeanor toward us—left me unsettled. Something had changed in that previous phone call. He sat up straighter, stared at us more intently.

Things moved quickly after that. Two officers took us from the room, showed us into a police car, and drove us to the offices of the Counter-Terror police. There we were photographed, had our fingerprints taken, and were processed. It made me uneasy that the Counter-Terror police were dealing with us now.

Back at the police station, it became obvious as we waited that there was no way we were going to be allowed to remain in Turkey for a couple of weeks before leaving. From the snatches of conversations we could overhear, it seemed like our deportation was going to happen much, much faster than that. And we still had no lawyer, although our friend was working on it.

"Please," I asked, "may we at least get a notary in here so that we can give power of attorney to someone? Our lives are in Turkey. We've got a van, an apartment, bank accounts. Can we at least make some arrangements to have someone deal with them?"

"That should be no problem," said the chief, picking up the phone. "But I will need to check first."

Minutes later he gave us the verdict. "No," he said in a way that made it perfectly clear that there was no opportunity for discussion.

MY PHONE BUZZED. We had some news—our friend had found us a lawyer. Taner Kilic, a human rights lawyer who happened to be the president of Amnesty International in Turkey, had agreed to come. We texted Taner, and as time passed we sent him a few more texts urging him to hurry. Finally he arrived. But as soon as he learned we were being held as a threat to national security he looked for a quick exit. I had only gotten a few minutes with Taner—he was trying to leave but I was trying very hard to hold on to the only legal help available. He gave me only one piece of advice: "Let them deport you, and then appeal from the US. If you appeal now, they may keep you locked up for the two weeks it takes to resolve." And then he was gone.

Ironically Taner Kilic himself was unjustly arrested eight months later. We could not have known it at the time, but the Turkish government would use this brief interaction with a lawyer we had never met before as one of the main ways to link me to terror groups.

"TIME TO GO. We're turning you over to Migration Management," the chief announced. "They are the ones who will give you more information about your deportation."

On our way out the door, I got a call back from the consular official. I told him about the latest development.

"Which center are they taking you to?"

"I don't know. Why?"

"It's rare for them to keep Americans if they're going to be deported. But one of the centers—Isikkent—is a lot less nice than the other. Let me speak to the governor of Izmir and see if he can help out somehow."

I could feel my throat tighten.

Two officers escorted us to a police car outside. There were no handcuffs, and we were allowed to sit together in the back, still clutching our cell phones. But the way the officers flanked us as we walked to the car and closed the doors firmly behind us told us that we were clearly under arrest.

"Excuse me, sir," I asked as soon as we started driving. "Can you tell me where you're taking us?"

"Isikkent," he said.

I reached out for Norine's hand. We drove in silence for a few minutes.

The car pulled over on a busy street. The officer in the passenger seat had just received a call.

"What's your home address?" he asked. "The governor has said we can take you back home to pack before we take you on to Migration Management."

As triumphs go, it was small. But it felt good. At least we could get some clothes, some important papers, and our laptops. It would make it easier when we arrived in the States.

We pulled back into traffic and the car started heading toward our home.

But whatever good feelings we enjoyed soon disappeared when the officer's phone rang a second time. I could hear the man's voice on the other end telling him to ignore the governor's request: "Bring them here NOW."

ISIKKENT IS A FEW MILES OUT from the city center, and even though the Friday evening traffic was heavy, the journey sped by. I pulled a battery pack out from my backpack and made sure Norine knew how to use it with her phone. If we were going to be split up, we'd need to stay in touch with each other as well as with home.

All too soon the car slowed and turned into the city's industrial area. The streets were empty. The only lights came from behind the fifteen-foot-high fencing topped with razor wire that surrounded the center.

As soon as the front gates closed behind us we were separated. Norine was taken away by a woman, I by a man to a small room inside.

"Empty your pockets," he ordered. "Pens. Shoelaces. Belt. Phone."

Phone?! This surprised me since we'd been allowed to keep our phones all day. Had we known, our first priority would have been to call our kids.

And shoelaces? Belt? What was this?

I handed over everything he asked for. I wanted to protest, but before I could speak he was patting me down and searching through my backpack.

Minutes later I was taken out of the room and into an office.

Norine was already there, standing in front of a desk. In her half smile I detected the same mix of emotions that I was feeling. Relief that we were together again, shock at what was happening. The guards stood at our backs.

SITTING AT THE DESK was a dark-haired man in his thirties, clearly unhappy to be stuck at work so late on a Friday night. When he looked at us he made no effort to hide his feelings.

I asked his name. "Melih."

"Please, Melih Bey," I said. "Will you let us phone our children? They're in the States and we haven't spoken to them yet."

"No."

"We need to let them know what's happening."

We were desperate. Norine joined in, "Please, just one quick call. We can call in front of you. Or let us give you the number and you call. Please. They will be worried. The youngest is just fifteen."

His stare was clinical. It was as if he was both fascinated and not unhappy that two Americans should have ended up in his office.

"No." He pointed to a paper on his desk: "Sign here."

I reached out to pick it up, but paused when Melih didn't move. "Can I read it, please?"

The same cold stare shot right at me. Then, with a shrug, he handed it over.

Both of us could speak and read Turkish well, but when it comes to legal matters, a lot of official documents in Turkey use old words and phrases that we don't know well. We huddled together and read the page, which contained the words "We understand that we have been informed of the reason for our deportation," followed by a list of various offenses. He'd ticked the box next to the one labeled *G-82—Threat to National Security*. This we already knew from earlier in the day.

Melih turned his attention to his computer screen, and Norine and I whispered our concerns.

"Do you think we should wait for a lawyer to see this? If we sign," Norine said, "does that mean we're giving up our right to protest? Are we going to kill off any chance of coming back to Turkey?"

I shook my head. "Remember what the lawyer told me? He said we need to be careful about protesting. If we protest now, before they deport us, they can hold us for a couple of weeks while the appeal is considered."

I could not imagine being in this place for two weeks.

"If they've decided to deport us, let's not get in their way. We can fight it from the US better than we can fight it here in a detention cell."

Norine agreed, and we both signed and handed the sheet back to Melih.

He exhaled as he examined it. Then the phone rang.

Melih picked up.

"I have it," he said. The voice on the other end was muffled, but spoke rapidly. After saying yes several times while staring at the page, Melih put the phone down and took out his pen and placed a tick in a second box.

Even reading it upside down, Norine and I knew exactly what it said: "Those who are a manager, member or supporter of a terrorist organization."

I felt Norine's fingers close around mine. She told me later that in that moment, fear wrapped itself around her heart.

Melih looked up at the two guards behind us. "You can take them now."

3 | LOCKED AWAY

WE WERE LED, ONE GUARD IN FRONT, one behind, back down the corridor and through a heavy metal door to the cells. Norine kept repeating, "Something's not right, something's going on."

All I could do was pray that we weren't about to be separated.

Every door we passed in the corridor was strong, solid, and shut tight. The guard leading the way unlocked the final door and pointed us inside. "We'll be back with some food," he said. "And don't worry about the noise you'll hear from next door. He's a bit different."

Norine and I exchanged glances. The sound of the key turning in the lock was heavy and dull.

We both looked around. The room was almost empty, with four bunk beds, a dirty tile floor, and two dirty sinks with a small bathroom off to the side. A window above the sinks had heavy bars across it. It was basic, but at least we were together and alone in it.

I stared at the toilet. Every place we'd ever lived in Turkey had included a typical Western toilet, the sort you could sit down on. This traditional Turkish style was different—a hole in the ground that you were supposed to squat over, and a little faucet attachment beside it for you to clean both yourself and the drop-toilet. I glanced at the little window and realized this was where the flies were coming in. There was no glass in the frame. I tried in vain to close the toilet door to keep them contained.

Within minutes another guard arrived with blankets, sheets, styrofoam boxes of food, and a couple of loaves of bread.

"Can we get some more drinking water?" I asked, looking at the four little water bottles.

"Not on the weekends. Do you need soap? I can get you that. And toothbrushes, a towel, and pajamas."

This was a help because we had no clothes other than what we were wearing and a T-shirt and hoodie in my backpack left from the recent beach trip.

We thanked him and opened the styrofoam containers. A tomato, a little wrapper of cheese, a bit of jam. Breakfast. The next box had rice and some vegetables.

"Norine, we haven't had anything since this morning, we need to eat something."

She quit after a couple of bites. I forced half the meal down. We were both exhausted from all the events and emotions of the day.

"Allahu Akbar!"

The sound of a man wailing in Arabic filled the room. It was coming from next door and his voice was so full of passion that he was almost screaming. It was dark outside by now and the single overhead light was dim. We looked at each other in silence. Norine's eyes were wide with fear.

I broke the silence. "I hesitated to tell you, but after what happened today it makes sense. I don't understand why, but I think God is involved in this, and that our time in Turkey is over for now." For the first time I explained to Norine about *It's time to come home*, the thought that I had wrestled with the last few days. Her first reaction was to ask, "Are you sure this is from God?" But as we talked it through she started to feel a sense of relief that God was in this sudden turn of events.

But it was still hard to wrap our minds around the fact that we really were on our way back to the US. Why would God allow this when there were so many encouraging things happening in our ministry? Besides,

God had told us in 2009 to prepare for spiritual harvest in Turkey. Were we really going to see it only from a distance?

The more we talked and thought about it, the worse we felt. We thought about one person after another whom we would be leaving behind. We were both grieving. The sense of being separated from all these things that I had poured myself into was so real I could almost feel it in my bones.

Norine was staring out of the window. After a few minutes she spoke up. "I think we should 'go with thanksgiving.'"

I immediately understood. A friend had sent us a message just hours before: "Don't look at all you've lost or everything that is difficult about today. Just be grateful."

Norine continued, "Let's remember all the good things God has done over the years in Turkey, starting with keeping us here for twenty-three years."

And so we did. We started listing all the things we could think of that we were grateful for. But for every memory that made us smile, the hardships surrounding it came to mind as well. It was as though a grace that had been there for years had suddenly been lifted. We'd seen so many victories over the years, but there had been a cost to each and every one of them.

IT WAS LATE. We were wiped out and needed sleep. "You know what's strange," I said to Norine as we made up the beds. "Usually when they deport missionaries they just throw out the husband and assume that the wife and any children will follow. But the deportation order is for both of us."

Norine slept that night like she always did, deep and sound. I tossed and turned in the bunk across the room, waking up every time the metal slot in the door clanged open and a flashlight shone through.

When the dawn call to prayer rang through the walls and open windows, voices from other cells started to wail along with it. I felt a chill run throughout my body.

Living in a Muslim country, we were used to the call to prayer coming from the mosques, but this felt different. Izmir is known in the rest of Turkey as Infidel Izmir. It was definitely cosmopolitan, and many people dressed like they belong in Milan or Miami rather than in a strict Muslim country. While headscarfs were increasingly common, it was still unusual to see a woman completely covered in black with only her eyes showing.

We had been told that Isikkent was the worst of the two centers, but my guess was that "worst" didn't relate just to the quality of the food or the standard of the bedding. It was also about whom they detained there. I suspected Isikkent must handle the more serious cases. And in Turkey in 2016, that could only mean one thing: ISIS. So I figured that if Norine and I were locked up with terrorists of the worst kind, that couldn't be good.

"HOW ARE YOUR LENSES?" I asked Norine when I finally heard her stirring. She never slept with her contact lenses in her eyes. She said they were sticking and wondered how she could last until Monday without any solution. I knew she could not manage without them.

In the daylight we located the cleanest-looking mattress and pulled it onto the floor so we could sit up straight. As we pulled out breakfast I reminded Norine of the bag of snacks our friend Ali had brought us the day before as we were being led to the police car. Our world had been turned upside down, but his act of kindness warmed our hearts now. We wondered if any of our friends even knew where we were.

"I'm concerned about the kids," said Norine as she stared at the uneaten food on the styrofoam plate. "Jordan will have told them about the deportation but they'll be expecting us home. When they don't hear anything by tonight and can't get through to us they'll start to worry."

On the way back from getting fingerprinted, we had sent a quick text to Jordan for his birthday, saying we were about to be deported and would be in touch when we knew more.

"Oh Lord, we have no way of letting our kids know where we are. Please help them. There is nothing we can do."

One prayer request led to another . . .

"But Lord, we also want to worship you in this place. We choose to praise your name . . ."

Lunch arrived—noodles in a sauce, some vegetables, and of course a half loaf of bread each. It would not be a meal in Turkey without bread.

BEING LOCKED UP behind a big, metal door in a foreign country, hearing the keys turn and the bolts slam for the first time, is sobering— you can't be sure about anything anymore. Now everything happens *to* you—it is a sudden loss of control and plunge into uncertainty.

Just when we'd exhausted all speculation about how our deportation might happen, the door's locks clicked and it slowly opened. "We are taking you for air," said a guard we had not seen before. "Come."

Norine looked as unsure as I felt as we followed him out of the room, down the stairs, and into a small courtyard outside that was blocked off by high walls. "You have twenty minutes," said the guard as he watched us from a chair in the corner.

"Look," said Norine quietly, pointing out several signs listing the rules of the facility. "There's Turkish, but this is Arabic, this is Russian. Farsi. Urdu. That's who we're in here with."

The rest of the day was spent back in the room behind the locked door. We prayed, we sang, we talked. Round and round we went with the same conversations. Our kids. The church. Our future. The only bright spot in leaving Turkey was that we would be closer to our kids. We asked every guard who came to our door when we were going to be deported, but all we got was "Wait until Monday."

Dinner arrived, and breakfast with it. We sat, we paced, we stared out the window into the darkness. Norine slept again, but just like the first night I was too wired to do anything other than doze fitfully.

Finally the door swung open for the morning window-and-bars inspection. Norine spoke up, "Do you have any more soap or shampoo so I could wash clothes?"

"Sure, do you want a bucket to wash them in?"

It was something to be thankful for. Norine busied herself with laundry as I paced from the window to the door and back again, dozens of times.

Norine was hanging a shirt on the window bars. "Isn't that the church van parked way over on the dirt road?" she exclaimed. "And look, there's Mert!"

At last, some good news. Our friends really did know where we were, and they were letting us know. The sight of people who cared, friends we would miss so much, made me cry. I loved these people and it hurt to have to leave them.

I turned to Norine. She was silent, her face free from emotion.

"Are you holding back?" I asked.

"No, my love," she said. "When we are on the plane leaving Turkey I'll cry."

WHEN MONDAY finally came around we got dressed in eager anticipation of something happening. After a whole weekend locked away, we were ready to go.

I stood staring out the window at the empty streets beyond the razor wire. The front gate was just out of sight, but I saw a man in a suit approach, heard him talk and recognized him as Robert, the consular official who had warned me about Isikkent. He left soon after, and I wondered if he had been turned away. As Robert wallked off I watched a car pull up, and a well-dressed couple I did not recognize got out and exchanged a few words with him. The couple marched toward the gate, but it seemed like they too were turned away.

We banged loudly on our door, hoping to get someone's attention, asking to see Melih Bey.

"I'll have to get permission," said a weary guard.

An hour later he walked us to the office. Melih sat behind his desk like he had before, but there was another man with him. He told us his name was Burak and he handled all the talking.

"What do you want?"

"We wanted to make sure you know we do not want to appeal the deportation at this time."

He paused. "Okay," he said eventually. "You can put that in writing. Something like 'I, Andrew Craig Brunson, want to return voluntarily to America. I am giving up all my rights.'"

I nodded. "You don't even have to deport us," I added. "Just take us to the airport and we'll get on whatever flight's available."

Burak winced and shook his head. "We have a procedure. Deportations are always from the Istanbul airport and the flight must be a direct one to the US. First, though, there is some official communication back and forth with Ankara. The paperwork should not take too long. A day or so. Maybe even by the end of today."

TUESDAY MORNING, the same well-dressed couple showed up outside, accompanied by a couple of church members. This time I could hear the man and the woman talk, and they were insisting that they had the right to visit us. I heard one of them say "lawyer." Were they trying to stop the deportation, not knowing we had decided to appeal only after we were Stateside? Without attracting attention from the guards below, Norine and I tried to motion to our church friends that we didn't want a lawyer.

Within a minute our door burst open and two guards were shouting at us. "What were you doing? Were you talking to someone on the street?"

"It is forbidden!"

"We're sorry, we did not say anything."

As they left, Norine and I looked at each other, hoping nothing would come of this. The last thing I wanted was for us to be separated as a punishment—and to be put in the same cell with one of our ISIS neighbors. We stayed clear of the window.

Our door soon opened again and a different guard came in. "You're coming to the office."

We followed in silence as he led us down the hall. Burak stared intensely at us. "Are you appealing the deportation? If so, you could be here for months."

Months? It was supposed to be two weeks. We certainly did not want to be here for months. We would appeal later.

"No," I answered. "We want to go to the States."

"Then write that you don't want to see a lawyer." He handed me a blank sheet of paper and glanced at Melih, who nodded back at him.

I picked up the pen and wrote what he dictated. "I want to return to America as soon as possible. I do not want a lawyer."

"Add that you do not want to *meet* with a lawyer."

I did what he asked, signed, and gave the pen to Norine. When she'd finished, Burak took the paper and handed it to Melih.

He gave it back to us. "Write down the time, 10:30."

When we'd done that, Norine spoke. "Is the deportation paperwork in from Ankara?"

Burak waved the guard to take us back. "We're still waiting to hear from them."

As soon as we got back in the room, we heard shouting from the street outside.

"Andrew! Norine! Are you there?"

A couple of guards were telling our friends and the couple to leave, but as they backed away I heard our friend shout out. "We have a lawyer for you! Andrew! We have lawyers but they won't let them in to see you."

I wanted to yell out and tell them that it was okay and that we didn't need a lawyer, but I did not want to risk getting in trouble. We sat, our backs to the wall, and held hands. Now they would have no excuse to keep us here. Soon we would be on a flight home.

But another thought intruded: Melih and Burak were not friendly men. We could not trust their intentions. Had we made a mistake?

That night we took a couple of mattresses and placed them side by side on the floor. For Norine, sleep was an escape—because she could sleep. But I was having trouble, and wanted to be close to my wife as the hours crept by. When daylight finally filled the room and Norine woke up, we quickly put the mattresses back on the bunks before the heavy door clicked open.

Surely we would see some movement today.

BY LUNCHTIME there had been no news. We had both had enough. We banged on the door and asked to see Melih again. This time he and Burak came into our room to talk to us.

"What is going on?" I asked. "Is there some problem?"

Burak looked away, but Melih carried on staring at us both. The silence that settled on the room was agony.

Eventually, Melih spoke, "Ankara will make the decision."

Norine drew in a quick breath. "What do you mean, they *will* make a decision? You mean it's not sure that we will be deported?"

He paused. "You will most likely be deported." He let the words hang in the air. "It's . . . 95 percent sure."

For the first time, a Turkish official was telling us we may not be sent home. I didn't want to think about what this could mean. I slumped onto one of the bunks, feeling weighed down.

Burak and Melih walked away and the guards took us out for air. We followed them in silence. Instead of pacing in the courtyard, we sat on a bench, quiet and subdued. The last thing I remember was my vision narrowing, fading fast. I felt my head roll back, and everything went dark.

4 | RIPPED APART

EVERYTHING HAD FADED. All my strength had gone. I couldn't even speak or shout out to ask for help. I was powerless as I tried to swim up through this fog, desperate to get back to consciousness.

Someone was standing over me. A guard, perhaps? I wanted to reach up and grab hold of his arm, but I couldn't. My body had locked me out.

I heard someone else shouting, but quietly, as if they were in another room. Was it Norine?

"I am NOT going to lose you! Satan, you can't have him!"

It was Norine, all right. I recognized her voice. I tried to break back through whatever this was that had washed me away from her. I had to get back to her, I couldn't leave, I fought from going under again.

I saw the colors and shapes gradually return. Norine was leaning over me, still shouting about not losing me, and a guard was staring at me. I could see the fear on Norine's face.

It took time, but eventually I could breathe more easily. I couldn't speak, my heart was still beating just as fast and I felt weak, but at least I was back. At least I was able to see Norine again.

I had been out for several minutes and was still too weak to walk on my own. Two guards half carried me back to our room, and I lay down on the bunk, soaked with sweat, drained and exhausted.

Burak came in and stared at me before delivering his verdict. "You don't look well. We're taking you to the hospital."

"No!" I was adamant that was not going to happen. Weak as I was, I was still aware of the risks of being separated. Once they split us up, who knew if they'd let us be together again? I did not want Norine to remain alone in the cell. "Just . . . let me sleep."

How long Burak stayed around I don't know, but when I opened my eyes again he was gone. I was cold and shivering, and Norine told me that she'd asked one of the guards for a heater, but it wasn't working. She piled blankets on me.

"Let's not complain," I said. "I don't want to give them any reason to separate us."

Burak came back soon after. This time he was insistent about sending me to the hospital.

"I don't want to go. I don't need it."

"It's not your choice."

I knew he was right, but I was desperate not to be separated. "Okay, I'll go, but please, let my wife come with me."

He shook his head. "I would have to send two extra police officers to guard her. No, you're going alone."

Within minutes I was being put in a police car. I was too tired to complain about being in handcuffs for the first time in my life. I was too weak to care that I was being treated like a criminal. I kept trying to sit up straight but finally slumped into the policeman next to me. At the hospital what little strength I had went into walking without stumbling, or talking to people when they asked me questions. I felt as ill and as weak as I ever had, but I did not want to give anyone a reason to keep me in the hospital any longer than necessary.

After an MRI they took me back to Isikkent, though without the handcuffs this time. They had realized I was in no shape to resist in any way. The hospital had found nothing wrong with me and offered no explanation for what had happened.

It was dark by the time I was returned to the room and left alone with Norine. Hearing the lock click on the door behind me was strangely comforting.

THE NEXT DAY was a blur of half sleep and daydreams. I tried to eat the food that they brought but had no appetite. When much of my strength had returned we tried to make a schedule to help pass the time.

We talked a lot in the beginning, but as the days slipped by we had less and less to talk about. We sat in silence—glad to be together, but with a growing sense of dread. We just could not talk with much enjoyment, or hope, or confidence about things that might now be in jeopardy—our children, ministry, future.

What remained was prayer and walking. These times became our focus, and as we walked in an oval, Norine often in front, me behind, we'd sing songs, try to remember verses, and pray. We varied our routine too, using the mornings to focus on things we were thankful for while in the afternoons we often prayed for our kids and the church. At night we'd try to get in the right frame of mind to sleep, often praying through the words of Psalm 23.

We were midway through one of our morning sessions when the door opened and a guard told us that Melih wanted to see us.

He was standing behind his desk when we entered. It was covered in some of our clothes from home.

"Your friends brought these in for you. You can take them if you want."

We started putting them into the empty bag that lay on the floor. The clothes and toiletries were all welcome, but when I saw my Bible I felt my heart race. I reached for it, so glad that finally we would be able to spend our time reading Scripture, but as my fingers brushed the cover, Melih reached out and pulled it away from me.

"No," he said, casually putting the Bible on a shelf behind him. "We won't give you this."

I was genuinely surprised. "We are Christians, we should be allowed to have our holy book. Why won't you let us have it?"

Melih shrugged. "You can only have books that we have provided for you. That's the rule here," he said, with a touch of disdain and cruelty.

As well as the desperate hunger for the Bible, I could feel the anger surging within me, but I knew we were at his mercy.

"Please," Norine said, much more calmly than I had spoken. "It's a Turkish Bible printed in Turkey. There is nothing illegal about it."

Melih sat down and waved us out.

HAVING A CHANGE OF CLOTHES was a relief. Not only did we smell better, but Norine found that doing the previous day's laundry helped kill a couple of hours each morning. Besides, the evenings were getting chilly now and we needed the extra layers. We had been trying to cover the broken window in the bathroom with a trash bag but that was not enough to keep the cold out.

My admiration for Norine grew. I had the seminary degrees and a PhD in New Testament. I had been preaching and teaching for years. But Norine seemed the stronger one at Isikkent. Over the years I had been like the hare, sprinting ahead and then slacking off, but she was the tortoise, every day setting aside time to pray and read the Bible no matter how busy or tired she was. Now she had a deep reservoir of time with God to draw from. It calmed me to be with her.

THERE WAS ONE TOPIC of conversation with Norine that didn't help me feel calm or peaceful. The state of emergency that Turkey was under.

Three months earlier, in July, there had been a failed attempt to overthrow President Erdogan. It had been totally unexpected, but in the aftermath Erdogan appeared to have a clear plan of how to respond to it. He publicly called the coup "a gift from God." He imposed a state of emergency and now ruled by decree. His grip on power was absolute, and tens of thousands had been arrested and could be held for years without trial. We had heard stories of people simply disappearing.

Norine was in the States visiting our kids when the coup attempt occurred, and I had joined her right after the coup. We'd had no qualms about returning to Turkey in August. The coup had nothing to do with us.

Now, we wondered how much the state of emergency had to do with our being kept here, with no access to legal or consular visits. This was a different Turkey than we had known.

"SO, ANDREW," said a policeman one day when we were out for air. "We're all wanting to know, when does the helicopter arrive?"

I had to look at his smirking face to realize that he was trying to make a joke. I ignored him.

"Your country has forgotten you, Andrew. Why is that?"

"The problem isn't *my* country," I said. "The problem is *your* country."

That comment aside, most of the guards weren't unfriendly to us as our time in Isikkent dragged on. Some were easier to talk to than others, and those we spoke with seemed genuinely confused about why we were still being held. We looked for opportunities to tell them about Jesus and to pray for some of them, knowing that most Turks have never met a Christian.

MOST OF THE TIME I took comfort in the grace and peace that Norine showed. But when we finished our twelfth nighttime prayer session, there was a tangible heaviness on us both. After almost two weeks of uncertainty, stress, and fighting in prayer, our words felt weak. The room was overpowered by our fear-driven thoughts.

Right from the start I had feared being separated from Norine. I hadn't wanted to give voice to the dark thoughts I'd been having—as if by speaking them out loud I would in some way make it more likely that they would happen. But by the end of day twelve I could not hold it all in anymore.

"Norine, what I'm really afraid of is that we will be separated. I won't know what's happening with you. And I don't know how I'll cope if I'm alone, without you. We don't know how long this will go on, or where it will end."

47

Norine wrapped her arms around me. The silence stretched out. What could she say? We lay on the mattresses we'd placed on the floor, holding each other.

NORINE DID NOT TELL ME at the time, but she was actually concerned that we might not be getting out anytime soon and was bracing herself. Was it possible we would simply disappear into the Turkish prison system as was happening to others? Would we ever see our kids again? Could it be that God wanted us in prison so that we could share about Jesus with the people there? Would the spiritual harvest that God had shown us for Turkey actually start in prison?

But she kept these thoughts to herself, not wanting to worry me.

WE WERE BOTH QUIET the next day. As we both sat on the mattress, picking at the food, Norine shook her head.

"I'm sorry," she said, sending me a half smile. "I'm at the end of myself today. I don't have anything left to say."

"It's okay. We've said everything already. What else can we say?"

We did not walk or pray as usual that morning. We both just sat on the floor as the hours passed.

"I'm picturing just sitting before God. He's quiet and I'm quiet, but he knows I'm there," said Norine at one point. "It might help you to do the same. No need to say anything to him. Just sit in his presence. And wait."

We were just as quiet when we were taken out to the courtyard later that afternoon. We sat together on the bench.

Norine kicked at a stone with her foot. "This has been my most difficult day. I'm really struggling."

A few minutes later she spoke up again. "Do you know what today is?" I shrugged.

"It's my mom's birthday." Norine smiled sadly. Her mother had died years earlier.

The doorway into the courtyard opened and a female police officer came in with Burak. I wouldn't have paid them any notice, but I was sure that I heard Norine's name mentioned. The moment I did, I felt my body surging with adrenaline.

The woman came over and stood in front of us. "We're releasing you," she said, looking straight at Norine.

"Wait," I said. "What are you doing with her? You're deporting her?"

"No, it's just an order for her release."

I looked at Norine. She looked just as confused about it all as I did.

"Well," I said, "can I go too?"

"No. We're taking her to the hospital now to be checked. When she comes back you can see her while she collects her things. Then she'll leave."

The next minute, Norine was gone.

I was taken to the cell and locked away on my own for the first time. I started pacing. I was relieved for her, so glad that she was finally being released, and glad that someone outside would finally be able to fight, but I was terrified as well. I could feel my throat start to close and my heart race. How was I going to cope now that the one thing I had been fearing all along was about to happen?

The room felt all wrong.

As I steeled myself, and prayed desperately, I resolved to dedicate this time to God, to sing songs of praise and worship, to focus on trusting and holding on to God. I wanted to make good choices. I wanted to get through whatever was coming as well as I possibly could.

I knew I needed to think clearly too, not be paralyzed by fear. So even though my breath felt fragile and my hands were shaking, I reached in the trash bag for some of the styrofoam plates we'd eaten off and used my fingernail to scratch the passwords to our various online accounts, as well as a list of all the people I could think of who might be able to help me get out.

The lock turned in the door and Norine was back in the room.

"You have ten minutes to get what you need," said the guard. "Then you can say goodbye."

The minutes sped by in such a rush. I had a headful of things to say, but no time to say them.

"Fight for me," I said as the guard moved her toward the door. "Fight for me."

The guards let me go with Norine to the main office. Burak was waiting there, and as they processed her, had her sign papers, we divided her things out from mine. When they started to pull her away Norine turned to argue with Burak. "Wait, I want to stay with my husband. Please let me stay."

Burak dismissed her. "No, that's impossible. You need to leave."

"Why can't I stay? I don't want to leave him. Let me stay with him."

Burak ignored her and nodded to the guards to hurry her out. Before she was out of the door we hugged one last time.

Hearing her say those words meant so much. I knew what it cost her to risk not being released. When she'd been so low that day and the night before, the choice to stay with me was beyond hard. And I also knew they would not listen to a word she said.

"I love you!" I shouted as the guards pulled me down the corridor to my cell. "Keep fighting, Norine!"

"You know I'm going to storm heaven and earth for you."

The door clanged shut and locked. I was all alone.

I ran to the window and looked through the bars. I could see her standing on the street. I waved one last time.

And then she was gone.

AFTER I BACKED AWAY from the window, I went through our usual routine of singing, praying, and reciting Scripture, trying to convince myself that this wasn't so very different after all. I got into bed, dreading the long night.

It must have been midnight when I heard footsteps in the corridor outside. Instead of the usual routine where the hatch opened and a guard shone a flashlight in, the lock clicked, the door opened, and the room was suddenly full of light.

"Gather your things," said the guard. "You're leaving."

"You're deporting me?" I felt a whisper of hope inside.

"I don't know. All I know is that you're leaving us right now."

Burak was waiting for me in his office. He looked tired, like he was in no mood for a discussion. "We just got an order to transfer you to another facility. Let's go."

I followed him out into the night.

PART TWO

5 | ALONE

THEY LIKE TO TRANSPORT YOU AT NIGHT. When the roads are deathly quiet and dark, that's when the authorities move you. It's more intimidating that way.

I was not in a panic—I was numb. Sometimes when bad things happen to me, part of me locks down and it's almost as if I'm an observer, sitting outside and watching myself from a distance.

At first I tried to keep track of the route we were taking, but as we left the lights of Izmir behind us and headed up into the darkness of the mountains, I gave up. All I could do was sit back and pray that somehow Norine would be able to find me.

Before I left Isikkent, Burak had called me into his office. He mentioned a name I had never heard before—a deportation center called Harmandali—and told me that he had received an order to transfer me there right away. He was annoyed because I was making him miss a soccer match that was on TV.

"What about my wife? Will someone tell her? She has to know. Please!"

Burak had always been less cold than Melih, but as I pleaded with him to contact Norine, he brushed my words aside and sent me out.

An hour after we left Izmir the car finally slowed. We pulled off the smooth tarmac. Suddenly I recognized where we were as we drove by the apartment of some of our closest Turkish friends from the church. I had eaten there several times. Now I was going by in the dead of night, so close, and yet they had no idea. We bumped along a rougher road for several miles. It was too dark to see the building properly in the distance, but when we finally stopped I could clearly make out metal gates, a security booth, and a handful of police waiting.

Inside, after I'd been taken through airport-standard security, a group of guards upended my backpack onto a table. When a gray-haired hawk of a man came in they all snapped immediately to attention.

Everything the old man said was delivered in a loud, impatient bark. "Don't give him that!" he said, pointing at my watch. "Or those"—he gestured toward my glasses. When the guards picked up the small plastic cross that Norine had left me at Isikkent, the old man's eyes grew wide. "Take that away. Don't give him anything."

I was led in silence to a room down on a lower floor. Once the metal door was locked shut behind me, I looked around. There were three bunks but no one else inside. Dirty sheets but no blankets. A Western-style toilet that didn't flush. A window with bars.

Without warning the lights went out.

From the street lamp outside I could just about make my way around the room. I gave up trying to find a light switch after a few minutes and gathered all the pillows and piled them around me as I lay on one of the beds.

I was shivering with cold, my eyes peeled wide. But inside I was numb. I'd felt that way ever since I'd left Isikkent.

As I lay in silence, the questions came. Like a plague of locusts they attacked my mind.

Will Norine find me here?

What happens if she doesn't?

What happens to me if they deport her?

What happens to me if they don't deport me?

I tried to block them out. I tried to distract myself, to pray or re-member the songs we had sung together at Isikkent. But it was no use. The best I could do was inhale the scent of Norine that still hung on my clothes, and wait.

THE LIGHTS CAME ON early the next morning. Soon the guards were banging on the door, shouting that it was time for me to get up. Minutes later the door crashed open. A short, stocky man in uniform yelled at me. "Get out here. What are you waiting for? Why aren't you ready?"

"Please," I said, holding up my hands. "Stop yelling at me. I don't know any of the rules. What am I supposed to be doing?"

"Get out."

Outside my room—my cell—were several guards. I had no idea why I needed so many, but they escorted me across the corridor to a room where there was Turkish tea and bread on a table.

One of the guards nodded at the food. "You want to eat here or go back to your room?"

I was so stressed that I couldn't even think of eating. "I'm not hungry at all," I said. Seconds later I was back in my cell. The door slammed. The lock turned. I was alone.

The window was low enough for me to look out, but the view was nothing like it had been in Isikkent. Back there at least there were streets and cars and once in a while a person to look at. In Harmandali there was nothing but scrubland, a mothballed construction site nestling beneath some hills, and way off in the distance, a thin strip of sea. I had never felt so far away from Norine.

I stared out the window, searching for a sign of life or some activity that might help distract my mind, but there was nothing to see. Hours must have passed as I watched, and still nothing happened.

I was in the middle of nowhere.

And I was in solitary.

AS THE DAY WORE ON the challenge of keeping my anxiety in check became increasingly difficult. Just before Norine had left we agreed that I would always hang a certain T-shirt in the window of our room in Isikkent so she'd know I was still there. The thought of her arriving and seeing the window empty tore me up.

I'd hear sounds in the corridor outside—guards shouting, doors slamming—and my heart would surge. I'd stare at the door, readying myself for the moment that it swung open, or holding my breath until the moment I was sure that the guards had gone.

I remembered the thought about how it was time to come home. In just over two weeks I'd gone from weeping because I *had* to leave Turkey to weeping because I *couldn't* leave. I had gone from begging to be allowed to stay in Turkey to pleading to be allowed to leave.

I thought about everything that we'd done in Turkey and the price I was now paying.

I thought about my kids.

I thought about my wife.

I thought about a song I had not heard for years—"Driving Home for Christmas" by Chris Rea. The chorus started playing in my mind, on endless repeat. It was taunting me, mocking me. Was I really going to be kept here until Christmas? Was I really facing another nine weeks of being locked up in solitary confinement? Could I even cope?

I had no control over where my mind went next, and with each shift in focus I could feel the panic ratchet up a notch.

At lunchtime my door opened and I was given food. I wasn't taken out of the room like before, but the styrofoam plate was brought to me. "You're high security," said the guard. "So you don't go out." *High security? Why would I be high security?* It didn't matter where I was fed, I could not eat. My stomach was twisted tight, my throat was locked.

It was the same with sleep. I knew my body needed it, but I could not sleep. Throughout the afternoon I tried to lie down and close my eyes. But every time I felt myself starting to drift, a massive surge of adrenaline would startle me awake and my heart would race once again.

The cell was its own torture. It was just me and a bed. I did not have a chair, and I could not sit easily on the bunk because of its low height. So I either lay on the bed, or stood, or walked. There was nothing to do, no reading, no writing, nobody to talk to. On its own this would have been enough to drive me mad. But with the added weight of fear it was overwhelming.

Piece by piece I could feel myself falling apart.

In the moments I was able to think clearly, I forced myself to focus on a single question: What am I going to do to stop myself from going crazy? I feared that if I let my mind wander too far then full-fledged panic and a total meltdown would follow.

I walked up and down the room and prayed, forcing myself to focus on God in order not to lose control. For the first time I realized that I was in the hands of a dreadful, malevolent spiritual power. The dread of this welled up inside of me and gripped my heart. I felt weak and powerless, a man alone, held captive by a vast, dark force.

All that day there grew within me an aching realization that this was now very, very serious. Maybe they were never going to let me go.

SOMETIME IN THE AFTERNOON of my first full day in Harmandali, a guard told me that I had a visitor.

Hope surged inside me. I jumped to my feet. "Who? Is it my wife?"

The guard shrugged. "I don't know. But you are to come with me now."

Norine was standing in the same area I had been processed.

As soon as I hugged her, I started sobbing.

I struggled to catch enough of my breath to finally be able to talk. "Look at what they've done to me, Norine. Look at me."

She held me closer. "It's okay, my love. I've found you now. I'm here. But we haven't got long, so I need you to listen to me."

All the time I'd been in my cell I'd been willing time to speed up. Now, with my head on my wife's shoulder, inhaling the scent of her hair, I begged time to slow down.

"I've been talking to people constantly since I got out. Your parents put me in touch with a group that specializes in this kind of case— fighting for Christians who have been locked up in the Middle East. They're very good and they say they're already asking political leaders from around the world to contact the Turkish government quietly. They're going to help get you out. And maybe that's why they've transferred you here—this is where most people are deported from."

Hearing Norine's voice, feeling her arms around my shoulders, and knowing she was fighting for me calmed me down.

But then it was over. A guard separated us. The door to freedom was right there, but only Norine could go through it. For the briefest moment I fantasized about breaking free and running out. But where to? I would be caught in no time.

I was led away. A minute later I was back in my room.

Alone.

6 | HOLDING ON

I AM NOT JUST CRYING, I AM SOBBING.

I am standing in front of a solid wood door with metal bars across the window. Even if it wasn't locked I would not be strong enough to open it. I am five years old, maybe six, but I know three things with absolute certainty. I know that the reason why I am being bullied is because I am the only foreigner in kindergarten. I know that eventually the principal will get tired of my noise and give in to my demand to phone my parents and ask them to come get me. And I know that my parents will say no.

After I was transferred to Harmandali, memories of my early years in Mexico began to surface. My parents had moved there as missionaries just after I was born. As part of their ministry they took in around twenty Mexican young people every year to live in our home while they finished high school. It was like a large, extended family—very large, since I was also the oldest of seven kids. At the same time, to be the only Americans in a small city brought a lot of negative attention for me as a young boy, and for much of my early life I was an outsider. Like salt on a wound, these early memories intensified the pain I felt in Harmandali.

BUT THEY WEREN'T THE MAIN THOUGHTS that I was concerned with. The only contact I had was with the guards. Some were more talkative than others. From asking them questions I pieced together that Harmandali was mainly home to refugees and people from other countries who didn't have the correct papers. Most of them were Afghanis, Pakistanis, and Africans, all held there awaiting deportation. They were allowed out three times a day to eat and then go to a courtyard to get some fresh air and to smoke.

What most frustrated me was that all of the people held at Harmandali were free to leave at any time. All they had to do was agree to be deported, and they would be taken to an airport and put on the next plane home. Few of them did, however. They all wanted to stay in Turkey, or at least move on to a better country than the one they'd fled.

Not me though. I was the only person there who could not leave.

The guards were also perplexed. This had not happened to an American before. But in addition, there was something different about *my* case, and none of the officials who ran the place were willing to give me even a scrap of information about what was going on—if they even knew. Everyone from the guard at the gate to the director seemed to be nervously following strict orders about me. It was clear that Ankara was making all decisions—big and small.

I SPENT HOURS EACH DAY looking out the window. I figured out that the rooms on the other side of the corridor opened onto the courtyard in which people walked and talked, but I was glad to be facing the front of the building. It meant that I could keep a lookout for Norine. Just seeing our van let me know that she was still in the country, that I was not entirely alone.

She came every day. As soon as it was light I'd stand sentry, my eyes locked on the point in the far distance where she would come over the crest of a hill and follow the narrow road that snaked its way up to the parking lot opposite the center. I would see the van come up the final hill, then lose it from sight.

Norine wasn't always allowed in to see me. I'd wait, sometimes as long as two hours, desperately hoping that my door would soon open and a guard would tell me that I had a visitor.

Most days my door remained silent and locked. When she was not allowed in, Norine would drive to a spot across the valley and park for a while. She—and usually others from the church—would get out. Without my glasses I could only recognize people by their shape, but I knew they were praying for me.

I'd keep my eyes locked on the view outside until the van slowly drove away. Even though it ached not to be able to see and hold her, at least I knew that she was safe and still free. How I longed to be in that van driving away with her!

One day, just when I'd given up hope that I'd be allowed to see her, the door opened. A guard was holding a slip of paper, gesturing at me to come and take it.

It was a note from Norine.

They don't always allow me to come and see you, but I've been told that I can send you this note. I'm still being the persistent widow, and there are lots of new friends who care about you. I drive here and try to visit every day. Don't give up hope, my love. N

It was like holding a priceless work of art. I read it over and over. *Be the persistent widow for me*—this is what I had said to Norine the night she was released. Jesus told the story of an unjust judge who kept denying a widow's request. She was so relentless that he finally gave in. I knew that Norine was being relentless for me.

And so I became a watchman. I spent hours each day standing and staring, and there was something comforting about the task. She always came, and the anticipation of seeing the van approach always made my heart yearn the way our German shepherd would strain against the leash and pull with all his might to get to Norine.

Then one day she did not show up.

Immediately I thought the worst. *What has happened to Norine? Has she been rearrested? Has she been deported? Has she been in an accident?*

I felt myself unravel. All the gains I'd made from watching for Norine—all the comfort I'd found in the routine—vanished. Panic swept over me. My breathing shallowed, my heart surged, and my mind spiraled further and further down. How could I keep going if I was now completely on my own?

I stayed that way for two days. Isolated from almost all human contact by the regime above me, deprived of almost all sleep by my own body and mind, I had never felt so weak and powerless. I prayed day and night for her. It was only when I saw our van crest the hill on the third day that the fear subsided.

I was so grateful to know that she was outside that I didn't even think that she might be allowed to pass a note or visit me. But within a few minutes of her arrival a guard was at my door announcing that I had a visitor. I quickly grabbed the styrofoam plate on which I had "written" notes for my next visit.

Because I had no pen and paper, I had begun to keep styrofoam plates that were not too greasy and use my long fingernails to scratch out words—prayer lists, fragments of verses, questions to ask Norine, encouraging things I heard from her, so that I would not forget them and could read over them again and again.

As for my fingernails, they were long because the guards would not let me cut them.

I TRIED TO HOLD MY EMOTIONS in most of the time—focus, press in, don't lose it. But when I saw Norine, the person who loved me and comforted me, my guard would collapse and my emotions poured out. I couldn't help it. And after the scare of the past two days, I felt it even more.

Norine and I both knew that time was short, so we talked fast. She told me that the lawyer had warned her to stay low for a couple of days, which was why she hadn't visited.

"What about your visa? Is that okay?"

Norine avoided answering my question fully, telling me instead about the two groups that were now advocating for me, Middle East Concern and ACLJ—the American Center for Law and Justice, based in Washington, DC. "MEC wants to keep things quiet," said Norine. "They want to keep going with the letter writing, to lobby the Turkish leaders that way. Maybe that's the best thing to do while we wait for the presidential election in the States."

Our time was running out.

I had come up with a plan to communicate on the days Norine could not get in for a visit. If she or our friends parked on the first road in the valley it meant everything was okay, if on the second road then there was a problem. I told her how to work out which window was mine and that I'd hang a certain T-shirt up to let her know I was still here and had not been transferred.

That was a big relief to her. "Andrew, last week while I was waiting for permission to see you, a man yelled out one of the windows—in English. His voice was desperate. A few minutes later a police vehicle drove through the gate and left. I tried to see if you were the one in the back, but I couldn't tell. I was frantic because I did not get permission to visit and see if you were still here or not." She had been shaken by the event. Every day afterwards she would come, dreading that I might have disappeared into the system, and would not relax until she saw the T-shirt in the window.

The visit ended too soon. I went back to my cell and tracked the van as it rattled along the road and then paused just where she said she would. Our practice run worked. We had it down.

THE FIRST WEEK BLED into the second, and still I was locked in my cell all day. I forced myself to eat—doing it as a discipline for God. I had turned down the offer of being taken out to the courtyard for air. What was the point? I was high security, so I was alone out there just like I was alone in my cell.

Although Harmandali was a modern building, the water was often cut off. I was given a half liter plastic bottle of water at lunch and supper each day. I learned to keep these bottles and fill them whenever the water came on. Soon I had a collection, enough to take a bird bath. And when the little radiator was turned on, I would place the bottles next to it overnight to make the water a little less cold.

AT THE END OF THE SECOND WEEK I received the biggest encouragement of my time so far at Harmandali.

It started when I walked into the visitors' area. Norine was standing there ready to hug me. But she was not alone. Next to her were two dear friends from church, Korean nationals who were living in Turkey. I was surprised to see them, but Norine gave me a look that told me just to go along with it all.

We talked and prayed, and when at one point Norine gave me another hug, she whispered that the guards had let our friends in because they thought they'd come all the way from Korea to see me, not an hour or two down the coast in Izmir.

They had brought me some kimbap—a Korean take on a sushi roll that I absolutely love.

"They put your favorite in it," said Norine, pointing inside the bag to the layer of paper at the bottom. Beneath it I could see the faint markings of something printed. Again Norine gave me the *just go with it* eyes, and after we said goodbye I hurried back to my cell, desperately hoping that I'd be allowed to keep the bag.

I was, and as soon as the door was locked I carefully lifted out the kimbap. Hidden at the bottom was a thin book, barely forty pages long, called *Prayers to Strengthen Your Inner Man* by Mike Bickle.

Instantly I realized this book was more precious than gold to me. It was life. Finally I had some verses from the Bible that I could read, some prayers that I could say when my own words and thoughts were too fogged up with fear. I now had something that I could build my day around, and I started spending hours and hours each afternoon and evening pacing from the door to the window and back, reciting the verses and letting the book inspire my prayers. And when I wasn't holding it with my back to the door, I hid the book in my pile of clothes, hoping that whenever one of the regular and random room inspections took place, the guard would not be interested enough in me to look through my underwear.

I NEEDED ALL THE HELP I could get. As the days passed by and the effects of too little sleep and too little human contact accumulated, I found it harder and harder to keep myself steady. No matter how much I paced and prayed and meditated on the pages of my little book, I could feel myself slipping.

Scenes from my years in Mexico kept coming to mind.

Those days at the kindergarten were not the only bad memories from that time. We were the only American family in the city, and to make it worse I was a missionary kid as well, making me a double target. When I was in junior high, I'd often get chased by gangs of older teenagers, even young men in their early twenties, laughing and shouting and throwing whatever they could find at me as I sprinted home.

I lived in fear, but my mother always said that the troubles I faced on the street were making me stronger. She was right too. They did make me stronger, but in a hard-hearted kind of way. And worse than that was what those troubles did to my view of God. I began to believe that I could expect God to put me in difficult circumstances precisely so that he could toughen me up.

It was only a matter of time before I started to see the parallels between Mexico and Harmandali. I was a foreigner in both. I was isolated. I was locked up. I was kept from my family. And my authority figure who could save me—in this case not my parents, but God—was using the pain and the fear of the experience to toughen me up.

LYING IN MY BED in the darkness, I was trying to ignore all these thoughts when one night I heard footsteps in the corridor outside. My light flickered on. Nothing good ever happens at night in these places. I held my breath.

The door opened.

"Gather all your things," said one of the two guards who walked in. "We're moving you."

"No!" I begged. "Please! Don't move me."

My words were weak. I had no control. All I could do was what they told me.

I scooped up my clothes, desperate to make sure that the book stayed hidden in my underwear. I followed them to another room on a higher floor. It was almost identical to mine, an outer cell with a window that faced the parking lot, the hills, and the road that Norine drove down. But this one was better. There was a light switch on the wall and the view out front allowed me to see the guardhouse where Norine would enter. Had I just been upgraded? I started to clean the room and make the bed.

An hour later the same thing happened. Footsteps outside in the corridor. Door opens and guards tell me to get up and leave.

This time they took me back to my old room. I was even more confused, but there was no time for questions. There was barely time for me to sit down and get used to the darkness.

Once more the door opened.

Once more I was taken out into the corridor and up a flight of stairs.

Once more I stood before a door while the guard fished out the correct key and unlocked it. Only this time, the room was not on the side of the building that faced the front. It was an inner room, facing the courtyard.

My heart sank. I would no longer be able to watch for Norine. I would no longer know if she was still in the country. I would no longer get encouragement from seeing her parked in the valley, knowing she was there praying for me. Now I was even more cut off.

The head guard was in the corridor. I pleaded with him to let me have my old room, but he ignored me. There was nothing I could do but walk into the room and listen as the lock closed behind me.

I lay on the bed, shivering, whispering the question that came from the deepest ache within me.

"Where is my loving Father?"

I thought I knew the answer—that God just wanted to toughen me up some more. It was a terrifying thought. How much tougher did I need to become? How much worse did things have to get before God rescued me?

7 | JUST BREATHE

I LAY AWAKE ON THE MORNING OF NOVEMBER 4, 2016, watching the gray daylight slowly invade the room.

I felt more isolated than ever. This room had a light switch and the toilet worked, but I really didn't care. I literally felt sick. Finally I got up and shuffled across the room to the mirror. I stood in front and stared at the unshaven, ragged man looking back at me. He looked so sad and so wild that I had to turn away.

Soon a guard was banging on the door. When it opened and I looked into the hallway I saw a group of fifty or sixty people crowded together waiting to go to breakfast. I passed. I did not have the heart to leave my room. But when lunchtime came around I made myself join them, and found a seat at an empty table, ignoring the confused looks a few people were giving me.

Between the light switch, the mirror, and the communal dining I figured out that I had been moved to a floor for people of a lower risk category, but I could not understand why. At least, I couldn't until later on that day when I was taken from my cell to a visitor room where I saw Robert, the consular official.

"I'm sorry it has taken me so long to see you, Andrew. They've only just given permission for me to visit."

I was so relieved to see him. During my first week at Harmandali an officer had pressured me to write a statement saying I did not want

71

to meet with any US officials. I refused. After a couple of phone calls to higher-ups, he tried to persuade me again. I was indignant: "Your government has burned me once—I won't trust you again. Why would I sign such a thing? This shows what your true intentions are."

Burak and Melih had lied to me at Isikkent, leading me to believe that just meeting with a lawyer would keep us there for months. The paper they had me sign saying I did not want a lawyer to appeal my deportation was now being used to keep me from all legal help to appeal my detention. After this I wasn't signing any papers.

I thanked Robert, but told him that I was confused by what was going on. "I don't know why I'm here or what they're doing," I said, struggling to keep my voice from being overcome with emotion.

He was just about to answer when the door opened. A policeman entered, followed by a careful, reserved-looking man. He introduced himself as Hasan and explained that he was the head administrator.

Robert gave me a look that suggested I let him do the talking for a while. I listened as he asked them to return my glasses and also if he could give me some books, pen, and paper that Norine had sent.

The policeman tensed. "We should ask Ankara."

I could feel the opportunity slipping away, but Hasan shrugged. "It's okay. It shouldn't be a problem." He held out his hand for the two books that Robert had brought, flicked through them, and nodded. "Let him have the books. Whatever, it's not important."

I could barely take my eyes off my Bible, but like a starving man at a banquet, I wanted to take everything I could possibly get my hands on. "Please," I sputtered. "I really want to be moved to the front side of the building again. It's good for me to be able to see the sun. It's warmer and I can tell the time that way. It helps me . . . psychologically too."

"I'll look into that," he said offhandedly as he left.

Back in my room I stood in front of the window and let the cold breeze swallow me. I knew that I needed to pull out my prayer book and spend some time reciting Scripture and praying as I walked the room, and I was glad to finally have the treasures that Robert had brought me, especially my Bible, but I was still stuck in the same inner room.

I had been staring aimlessly out the window, not noticing that ahead of me, on the other side of the courtyard, was an office. A light was on and I could see Hasan, the man with whom I'd just been meeting.

I knew what I should do. I knew that I should keep quiet, not bother him or do anything that might upset him. But I could not hold back.

"Excuse me!" I shouted. "Sir!" He turned to the window and looked over at me. "Please don't forget about me!"

He nodded vaguely and turned his back on me.

An hour later my door opened.

Two guards were standing there. "Come," they said. "Bring your things."

I didn't ask why. If they were moving me somewhere better, that would be good. But if my shouting had been a mistake and I was about to be punished, then so be it. I was powerless to change anything.

THE NEW ROOM was on the same floor. It was for lower security inmates like the previous one, so I could control my own lights and stare at myself in the mirror. It was also at the front of the building, and it was higher than my original room, so I could see not only the road but also the parking lot and the guard booth at the gate.

Even before the door was locked shut behind me, I started to write in my new notebook.

"The kind God, the gentle God, the God who cares about my heart." This is what I am thinking, tears welling in my eyes, at the end of a difficult two or three days that really tested my heart—days when I expected that you would remove those things that I care about, strip me, to make me tough and bulletproof. But my heart screams, "I don't want to be tough! I want to be your little boy . . ." Thank you. I have pen and paper, books and a Bible. Glasses returned. This is the best room I've had—now I will be able to see Norine more easily. May I leave here knowing that as I walk through the valley of the wolves, you are with me, and that even in the presence of my enemies you are doing good things for me.

NOT ONLY WERE THINGS BETTER in my new room, but soon Norine was allowed to visit me most days. And not just for twenty minutes either—often for as long as a whole hour. It was a dramatic shift.

Whenever Norine was allowed to visit she would always bring news that she hoped would encourage me. "Andrew, the prayer has really taken off. I'm getting reports off to others, and they in turn are spreading it to their networks." Sometimes she brought letters from friends— words that they hoped would inspire me to keep going and emerge from this trial victorious: "Sing like Paul and Silas! Preach to everyone around you! Have a great time, just you and God!" I understood why they would write such things, but the truth was that spiritually and emotionally, I was struggling just to survive. Whenever I opened my mouth to sing, I would choke up.

So I was grateful to receive the letter that contained the most helpful advice: "Just breathe. Keep your eyes on God. That's all—no other expectations. Just breathe and you will come through."

It was just what I needed.

IT WAS GOOD TO HEAR that numerous members of Congress back home had contacted the US Embassy in Ankara, urging them to act. But I was worried that time was running out. The work that Norine and I had been doing in Turkey was so small by US standards, and we had no profile back home to speak of. Surely it wouldn't be long before people's interest drifted on to another worthy crisis, or they just stopped feeling sorry for a locked-up pastor and returned to their normal lives.

That wasn't the only clock that was ticking. Norine's visa was due to expire on November 10, and that reality had hung over me from the time we were separated. She was the only person who was allowed to visit me. The thought of her being forced to leave the country had plagued me constantly. I'd prayed for hours on end, begging God to intervene, feeling like he was a judge about to rule. As the deadline approached there were many twists and turns but still nothing solid. My mother even came over from the States a few days before the visa ran out, to be on hand in case Norine had to leave immediately. After a couple of visits she was not allowed to see me anymore and would wait in the parking lot until my arm came out from between the bars to wave at her.

At the last minute Norine found out that she had been allowed to remain in the country.

I was elated when she told me, but within a day I was down again— struggling with questions about faith, fears about people forgetting me, suspicions that I was going to be taken deeper and deeper into the Turkish judicial system so that God could toughen me up some more.

Even eating with the refugees was discouraging. Word got around that there was an American among them. They would ask in surprise, "What are you doing here?" What could I say? It was painful to even try to explain, and I often came back to the room downcast. Most of them had never met a pastor, and they were curious. Although very few of them spoke English or Turkish, I prayed for them, helped in any way I could, and answered questions about my faith. I would talk about God being kind and loving, about him being a father who loved his children. But there were small fissures of doubt in my heart. I was not as confident as I sounded, not as confident as I wanted to be.

ONE AFTERNOON I had just written in my diary, "Where are you, my Shepherd?" At that very moment I heard the tinkling of the bells announcing that the herd of sheep that often grazed outside was passing by. I walked over to the window. The sheep were walking up the hill, but only the dogs were with them. There was no shepherd to be seen.

How ironic! It twisted into my heart. Where was my Shepherd?

THE MORE TIME PASSED the harder it was to resist the temptation to put God to the test.

In my first few weeks at Harmandali I had asked God for three things: to see Norine more often, that she not be deported, and that he take me home by Christmas, when my daughter was thinking of getting married. He'd come through for me on the first two, but what about the third?

One day I sat down and wrote:

If I miss this I will be bitterly disappointed, I will be a broken man—and you will have done it. I fear what will happen to my trust in you. In the end of course you are not on trial. I know in the light of eternity this is trivial. But it will fill me with pain, and deep loss. How does my heart survive that?

I meant every word that I wrote.

Hours later, though, I was feeling different. I prayed and repented of what I'd written. Who was I to put God to the test?

I should remove from my heart any conditions on which God will pass or fail.

I WAS WATCHING from the window the day Norine walked across the parking lot for her visit. She waited just like she usually did to get permission from the guard at the gate, but for some reason this time she was not allowed in. I could not hear what she was saying, but from her body language it was obvious that she was feeling frustrated. The gate remained closed.

I watched her take a few steps away to the side and get on her knees. I knew she was doing it as a sign that she was praying for me, but watching her kneeling there on the concrete in front of a bolted gate, I felt the anger rise in me all the same.

I felt angry for days. Angry with the director. Angry with the guard. Angry with Turkey for holding me like this and causing my wife so much pain.

ONE DAY, WITHOUT WARNING, just as I was pacing my room, the words spat out from my mouth.

"Do you even exist, God?"

I started to weep.

I had failed.

How could I have gotten this low? How could doubts like this come to my mind? I knew that God had been involved in my life, but these doubts were so fierce.

"Papa! Save me," I prayed. "I'm afraid of my own mind and thoughts."

In the aftermath I decided that I needed to discipline myself to state some very basic truths.

Each day I made my declarations:

"God, you exist. You love me, and you are in this.

"I am a prisoner for the sake of the gospel of Jesus Christ.

"I am suffering for Jesus. This gives meaning to my pain. It is precious to God, and he will give me eternal reward."

I would also add, "At some point you will rescue me. You said, 'It's time to come home.'" I reminded God of this phrase so many times. By now I was clinging to it as a promise, and desperately hoped that it would be fulfilled soon.

ONE OF THE BOOKS I had been allowed to keep told the story of Count Zinzendorf, an eighteenth-century missionary. He was on a ship that was caught up in a terrible storm—a storm so vicious that the captain told the passengers that within two hours the ship would be on the bottom of the ocean.

"No," said Count Zinzendorf. "Within two hours the storm will have passed and everyone will be safe."

The captain was wrong. The Count was right. When the captain asked him how he knew, Count Zinzendorf explained that ever since he was a child he had heard the voice of God accurately in his heart.

The story took root in my mind.

How was it that Count Zinzendorf could be in the middle of such a stressful experience and still hear God so clearly? And why hadn't God spoken to me in that way?

77

Into my mind, quite unexpectedly, came the thought, *Seventeen days*.

"Wait, what?" I prayed. "Are you saying this, God? Is it possible you're speaking to me?"

Immediately a second thought came to my mind. *I will confirm it.*

That night I could not sleep. Seventeen days ahead was December 12. The thought kept pounding in my head. The next day I read through every note that Norine had brought me to see if the number appeared. I searched the Bible, but it seemed there were few verse seventeens that people quote. I was desperate, grasping. If I was wrong it would be a terrible letdown. But if I was right and God really had just spoken to me, I'd be home for Christmas.

A few days later when she visited, Norine looked hesitant.

"What is it?" I asked.

"Someone from church said that they think you're going to be released soon."

I tried to keep my voice calm. "Oh. Did they say when?"

"December 12."

My anticipation was growing.

It took another leap forward a couple of days later when Norine returned and told me about an email she'd received from a friend in Belgium. He'd written to tell Norine that he'd had a dream in which I was released in twelve days' time.

"Norine," I said, looking at the email, "he sent it yesterday, November 30. This means December 12."

She smiled and held me tighter. "Let's try to hold it lightly, my love."

8 | THE WOLF

FOR A WHILE I WAS ALMOST AT PEACE.

Almost.

But even as I walked away from meeting with Norine that day I could feel the fear. Yes, I now had something to hope for. But what if it didn't happen? What if I was actually speeding toward heartbreak, not release? Could I really be so sure that God was not going to crush me again?

The closer I got to December 12 the more stress I felt. A new front opened up in the battle, and each day I focused on fighting through my fear to reach a place where I surrendered myself to whatever God had ahead for me. As difficult as it was, I knew it was vital. And I knew that I was powerless to change my feelings. I needed God to help me. I wanted to be willing to say yes to whatever God wanted, even if that meant staying longer in Harmandali so that God's plans would be fully carried out. "With my will I submit to you," I declared, so many times. "May this cup pass from me, but I submit with my will. Don't look at my feelings, but at my words."

Each day was the same battle. Only when I'd finally reach this place of relative peace and surrender would I let myself anticipate life after being released. I journaled my thoughts on how the previous two months had shaped me.

> I will be more humble, I will be more gentle with those suffering or those who have doubts, I will speak more carefully . . .

I WAS LYING IN BED just before midnight on December 8, half asleep, when a female guard came into my room.

"Get your things. You're going to be deported."

For a brief moment I felt excited. Yes, it was four days early, but I'd already learned how slowly Turkish justice could move. Maybe this was the start of my release, the beginning of the end.

I got up and started gathering my clothes, then stopped. Something was wrong. Why come and get me at midnight? I'd already seen a few people deported from Harmandali, and all of them were released in the evening, taken to Istanbul overnight so that they could be flown out early the next day. "Am I really being deported? Are you sure about that?"

She shrugged.

I put down the T-shirt I was holding. "Would you go and find out, please? If I'm being deported I will leave a lot of this stuff here. But if I'm being moved . . ."

My voice caught in my throat, and the guard disappeared.

By the time she returned I was pacing the room.

"I'm not sure if you're being deported but we're moving you."

Panic returned. My heart was racing, my thoughts thrashing around within me. "What's happening?"

She said she knew nothing more than what she'd told me already. "Just pack."

I looked around me. In the seven weeks that I had been at Harmandali, Norine had been allowed to bring me almost everything I asked for, especially since the visit from the US consul. I had blankets and a pillow, toiletries, clothes, wet wipes to clean the cell, and several books, pens, and papers. It was more than I could fit in my backpack. I was fumbling around, trying to figure out what to do when two more guards came in.

"We don't know where you're going but we know you're going. So take everything."

Whatever was going on, it didn't sound right. I could feel myself starting to fall apart again, panicking about whether I was going to end up in a basement cell somewhere. And how would Norine know where I was? She'd found me before, but how much longer might it take this time?

The three guards hustled me out and I stumbled downstairs, my backpack overflowing with papers and clothes, my arms loaded with blankets.

As soon as I saw the two men in plain clothes with guns waiting by the front desk, I knew I was in real trouble. One of them, a man in his fifties, told me that they were police, while the younger guy—wearing tight jeans, a leather jacket, and a sneer—told me that they were here to arrest me. Before I could tell him that I was already under administrative arrest and awaiting deportation, he jabbed a finger at me.

"You're under judicial arrest now."

They had me empty everything I was carrying onto the desk and the young sneering policeman barked his orders at me, just like the gray-haired director had when I arrived. "Get that bag! Put some underwear in it. Put some socks in there too. And a toothbrush, but that's it. Leave everything else!"

I was numb again.

Too shocked to say anything, too fearful to even think.

I reached for an extra pair of pants and the brightly colored T-shirt that I'd hung up in the window for Norine.

"No! I said you've got enough. You're not taking anything else."

The guards brought out a box with the rest of my possessions that they'd been keeping from me—my passport, some money to buy a plane ticket when I was released, my watch, the little cross that Norine had left me the night she'd been released from Isikkent. It was small enough to hide in your hand, and I thought about the verse written on it: *We know that in all things God works for the good of those who love him.*

The words had never felt so alien to me.

I turned to the older policeman. "Please, will someone call my wife and tell her? She doesn't know."

I gave him the number and he called. I was begging Norine to pick up, but there was no reply. Eventually he shrugged, ended the call, and nodded at the younger officer to pick up my file that was sitting on the table. "Let's go" he said, pointing to the car waiting outside.

I WASN'T CUFFED in the back of the car, but as I sat next to the younger officer I was in no doubt that I was a prisoner. They ignored me all the way back to Izmir. As I made the customary visit to a hospital to confirm that I had not been tortured—the same one I was taken to when I collapsed in Isikkent, the same one that was just a few minutes away from my home, from my sleeping wife—they stuck close to my side.

A few blocks later the car pulled up outside a familiar building. It was just across from our old church building, and I had walked by it many times as it was being renovated. I hadn't known what the place was going to be used for, but as we waited in front of the locked metal gates while the older police officer banged repeatedly on them, I saw the sign. They had brought me to the new Counter-Terror Police Center.

Once we were let inside it took two hours to process and transfer me to the basement cell that I had been dreading all along.

The bars across the front side of the cell ran floor to ceiling. Around the three walls was a narrow concrete ledge, just wide enough to sit on, but too narrow to lie down on. There was no bed, no mattress, no sink or toilet.

It was too dark to tell who was in the cells opposite. It was too cold and too uncomfortable and my heart was racing too fast for me to sleep. All I could do was lie on the concrete floor, wrapped in a blanket, and shout silently at God.

God, what are you doing? What are you allowing to happen? I'm supposed to be released on the twelfth, but here I am in this dungeon. How long will it be until Norine finds me? What is going to happen to me?

THE MORNING TRAFFIC was rumbling in the street overhead when I was taken from my cell. I was disoriented, not thinking straight from the combination of no sleep and too much adrenaline. But I did what

I was told. I stepped into the car when directed, and gave the officer Norine's cell phone number as we drove.

"Get your lawyer," he ordered her. "He's being taken to the Izmir courthouse right now for interrogation with the prosecutor."

I didn't get to hear what Norine said in reply. The officer didn't wait to listen. He just hung up. The rest of the drive was in silence.

AS SOON AS I WALKED into the courthouse and was escorted to the corridor outside the offices of a prosecutor named Berkant Karakaya, I could feel the tension. In addition to the two police officers who had escorted me, there were several men with submachine guns—bodyguards for Karakaya's boss, the chief prosecutor, Okan Batu.

I'd not heard of him before, but I knew the reputation of the office. Infidel Izmir may have been the home of the Turkish opposition, but it was exactly the kind of place that an ambitious prosecutor could come to and make a name for himself by aggressively pursuing those the government frowned upon.

I stood, weary and silent, and waited. For a while I let myself imagine that this might be the final twist before I was released. The more I thought about it, the more I believed that my release should be happening. After all, I was a citizen of a NATO ally, had been held for sixty-three days without access to a lawyer, and had been permitted only two visits from a consular official. Politicians in the US and other countries had been asking for my release—including Senator Bob Corker, who had met with the Turkish ambassador in Washington, DC, and handed him a letter to give to President Erdogan. It had been signed by seventeen senators and urged him to act. Erdogan had let loose, insulting President Obama after the election, but with President-elect Trump just weeks away from the inauguration, wasn't it about time he started making nice with the US?

It seemed to me that this whole thing should have been an embarrassment for Turkey. Wouldn't it be so much easier for them if they could just get rid of me quietly? And if that was what they wanted, then what better way than to wheel me out before a tough prosecutor, have him question me and acknowledge that there was no cause to hold me, and send me home?

"Andrew!" I looked up and saw Norine farther down the corridor. There were too many men with too many weapons between us for her to get close, but she stood and placed her hand on her heart and tried to smile. "This is how God is going to get you out!"

Before she could say anything else I was taken into Karakaya's office. A Turkish woman sat next to me and introduced herself as Suna, the lawyer Norine had arranged for me. She had keen eyes that scanned the room as she spoke.

We had about two minutes for her to explain what was going to happen. She pointed out my prosecutor and explained that he was the one who would ask me questions.

The minute Okan Batu walked in and sat next to his deputy, the room fell silent. Not just quiet, or hushed, but the kind of silence that makes you scared to breathe.

Turks—especially nationalists—like to identify with wolves. It's not unusual to see soccer fans and street demonstrators pinching their ring and middle fingers with their thumbs like a wolf's snout, their first and pinky fingers stuck up like the ears.

Okan Batu was the alpha wolf they would all obey.

Suna shifted in her seat. Nobody dared to speak. All eyes were on Okan Batu.

And his eyes—filled with pure hatred—were fixed on me.

"Andrew Brunson," said my prosecutor. "You gave a speech in October 2013 praising Fethullah Gulen."

It took me a moment to process his words. Like everyone in Turkey I had heard of Fethullah Gulen, the exiled head of the Gulen movement—an Islamist group that had started schools in over 170 countries. Gulen and Erdogan had been allies of a sort for many years, but when police and prosecutors conducted a corruption probe in 2013 that snared people close to Erdogan, including his son, Erdogan went on the warpath against everyone associated with Gulen. Three years later,

Fethullah Gulen was accused of being behind the failed coup, and his supporters made up the bulk of the tens of thousands of people who had been rounded up and locked away.

I couldn't remember my preaching schedule from 2013, but I knew for a fact that I'd never said anything praising either Fethullah Gulen or his movement. I tried to steady my voice and avoid looking at Okan Batu as I replied. "I've never met a Gulenist in my life, sir. And I've never spoken in support of them. Please, tell me what meeting I was at when I supposedly said this."

I've spoken Turkish for years, and people never have trouble understanding me, but I may as well have been speaking in code. He stared at me, then carried on with his questions, ignoring mine. "Have you ever been to the Zaman newspaper building?" This was a Gulenist newspaper.

"I have never been there. I don't even know where it is."

"Have you been preaching in Kurdish?"

"No! I don't speak Kurdish. I don't support Kurdish separatism and I don't support separatism in any way. I believe in the indivisibility of the Turkish land."

After a pause, Okan Batu spoke. "What do you mean by that?" Everybody knew what I meant. The indivisibility of the land is a hot topic in Turkey where the PKK, the Kurdish separatist group, had been fighting for their autonomy for years. I was being honest when I said I didn't support that in any form. But that wasn't good enough for Okan Batu and his eyes blazed even more fiercely. "It's not just the land that has to be united, it's anything else that could cause divisions among Turks."

I knew then that I was in danger. He was talking about me as a missionary, putting me on par with the forces that were trying to destabilize his homeland. To my mind, Christianity could only mean good things for Turkey. To a man like Okan Batu, a nationalist Muslim determined to repel all outside forces, my faith made me a clear enemy.

"Please, let me go home. I have never done anything to hurt Turkey. I was arrested so that I could be deported. Please, let me go home to the US."

My prosecutor held up his hand. "No," he said quietly. "I think there are enough reasons to keep you while we continue our investigations."

Suna turned to me. Her face was grim.

I whispered to her, "They're going to put me in prison, aren't they?"

She was not one to give false hope. "You will go before a judge, so there is still a chance. But yes, he will send you to prison."

Almost immediately I was taken to wait in another corridor outside a judge's office. Norine found me, and though we were separated by two glass doors, she stood where I could see her the whole hour I waited. When I placed my hand on my heart, she did the same. It was our way of saying "I love you."

Eventually I was taken before the judge, who looked at me and frowned. "What do you have to say for yourself?"

"I know what questions they just asked me but there were no formal charges made. How can I defend myself when I don't even know what the charges are against me?"

The judge stared with haughty indifference.

"Please," I begged. "I haven't done anything. Please, just send me home."

He looked away. "Send him to prison."

I WAS TAKEN BACK to the corridor to wait while they decided which prison to send me to. Norine was there, beyond the glass doors, hand on her heart again. My mom had arrived too. They were both pale with shock, their faces heavy with sorrow. Mom held her arms out in front of her, rocking them from side to side like she was holding a baby. Some of the bodyguards and police standing around me pointed at her and mocked.

The noise around me, the people jostling and laughing, it all faded away. I heard someone tell me that they were sending me to Sakran, but the name meant nothing to me. All I had was this panic, this fear, this pain of being so close to my wife, and yet not being able to touch her.

The two policemen who had been by my side all day moved me down the corridor toward the stairwell. I checked to see that Norine and my mom were following behind.

One of the officers stopped us. "Go ahead," he said, pointing at Norine. "You have one minute."

I felt Norine put her arms around me. I clung to her neck.

I started crying. "They're sending me to prison, Norine. Please go public and fight for me."

"I'm going to fight for you. There's an appeal coming up on Monday. It's the twelfth. We'll appeal it and maybe they'll release you, my love. The twelfth, remember?"

The twelfth? That all seemed like it belonged to another lifetime.

The tears were coming faster now. It was hard to speak, the words getting stuck in my mouth, mixed with tears and gasps for breath. "Norine, I'm going to prison . . . I'm going to prison." The policeman pulled me away. I looked back one last time before we turned a corner, and then I was gone. They walked me past the basement cells, photographed and fingerprinted me again. Then they put me in the back of the police car.

I sat, stunned by everything that had just happened.

The wolf had caught me.

PART THREE

9 | THE FIRST NIGHT

AS SOON AS THE CAR DOOR SLAMMED SHUT, the panic that had been surging inside me died down.

In its place was . . . nothing.

I was numb again. A dead man being driven through the city's dark winter streets, watching the alien world beyond the glass.

It took longer to reach the new prison than it did to get to Harmandali. Mile after mile we drove, me in the back seat of the car that smelled of stale cigarettes and sweat, the same two officers up front saying nothing to each other. In the whole drive there was just one interaction between us. "You have lived here for so many years. Did you really think you could work with refugees and not have problems? How could you be so stupid?"

I didn't bother to answer. There's a lot I could have said, but I was emotionally exhausted. And what would be the point? They wouldn't care anyway—I was just another prisoner to transport.

I sat motionless, my eyes closed. I could feel a massive spiritual storm starting to build, more intense than anything I had ever experienced.

Within minutes I was surrounded by a demonic whirlwind, a furious darkness swirling around me. This was not emotional turmoil—I could feel the evil.

The drumbeat of a new thought started up in my mind. *I am Job. I am Job. I am Job.*

In the Bible, God handed Job over to Satan to be tested, to see whether he would remain faithful in the midst of intense suffering.

In that moment I *knew*—God had turned me over! God had changed his mind, removed his protection in order to achieve some higher purpose, but at my expense. No, this was not just persecution, it was something else.

My heart was a morass of fear, shock, and anger: *How could you betray me like this, God?*

The car turned off at the Sakran exit, just a few miles before Pergamum. It was fitting. Pergamum—the city that Jesus had identified as the place of Satan's throne.

SAKRAN PRISON is not really one prison, but seven. It's a campus spread over a space the size of one hundred football fields and it's home to ten thousand inmates—murderers and revolutionaries, subversives and psychopaths, women and children.

I was taken to prison T4 and placed in a cell with bars—a cage really—until they were ready to process me. I was fingerprinted and photographed again, sent through metal detectors, then strip-searched. "Take your clothes off. Squat. Cough."

At one point a guard brought in the few items I had been allowed to bring from Harmandali.

I did not have much with me—the young sneering cop had kept me from taking clothes except what I was wearing, some extra socks, and underwear. I had grabbed my Bible. Now I watched helplessly as they took it away.

I LEARNED QUICKLY that compared to Sakran, Harmandali was like a resort. Sakran was a high-security prison, and everything about it felt different. The gates were higher, the windows smaller, the corridors broken up every few feet by another heavy metal door that had to be unlocked.

The guards were different too. At Harmandali some of them had shouted and cursed at the inmates while others were more sympathetic. But all of them were civilians. They'd slouch in doorways and some of them would even talk to you if they were feeling good. In Sakran the guards were more intense. There was no friendly chitchat, and when they gave commands they expected immediate obedience. Their eyes were full of suspicion, and as they moved about the prison it was always in groups, never alone.

There was no flexibility and little or no communication. I knew nothing about what was going to happen to me. I felt weaker than I had felt at any point in my life. I felt exactly the way they wanted me to.

The feeling of numbness stayed with me. I stood when I was told, walked on command, and paused in silence while the guards unlocked the door of the cell I was placed in. It was like it all was happening to somebody else.

The guard stood on the other side of the heavy metal door, looking at me through the small slot that could only be opened from the outside. "You're going to be here over the weekend until we decide what to do with you."

I looked around. Every part of the cell was filthy—the floor, the sheets on the bunk bed, the bag of bread covered in thick, green mold hanging from the barred window, the squat toilet covered in human filth. I had no appetite and couldn't imagine myself sleeping, but I knew I needed to drink. I was concerned that the tap water would make me sick so I asked the guard for a bottle of water.

"No," he said, turning to leave. "It's the weekend."

I hadn't been on my own all day, not since the guard took me out of the concrete cell in the Counter-Terror Center. The silence troubled me, and I tried to fill it by preparing mentally for a few days in complete isolation. I'd been through it before at the start of my time in Harmandali, when I had no books, no Bible, nothing. But this was different. The stress was greater. I was accused of terror crimes and held in a high-security prison. Being alone wasn't the worst thing possible. What if I ended up with some real criminals? How would a terrorist react when he found out he was sharing a cell with me? I knew I would be the only American, the only Christian, and certainly the only missionary. I had no idea how to even begin to prepare for a situation like that. No matter what I did, I knew I could be a target.

I found the cleanest of the dirty sheets, pillows, and blankets and prepared a bed. I was physically exhausted after no sleep the previous night and the horrible day but I paced the room. Even though I felt betrayed by God, I knew I had no choice but to look to him and try to hold on. My prayers were short, simple, and repetitive. I could only say, again and again, "Jesus, help me."

AN HOUR AFTER I was locked inside, I heard the many door bolts and locks open. The guard was back with a colleague. "Come with us," he said once he had opened my door. "The director wants to see you."

As I walked into his office the director frowned at me, like he was genuinely trying to figure me out. "Why are you here?" he said after I'd waited in silence, standing before his desk.

"I'm a pastor. I didn't do anything."

The frown dropped, replaced by a vague smile. "Is that so? You're with the FETO group, aren't you?"

"No! I've never even met a Gulenist in my life."

The director looked down at a paper on his desk. "Well," he sighed, "that's what you're in prison for. I'm going to send you to a cell now. There's one on C Block."

The fear lurched within me. "You have to be careful who you put me with. Some people could really dislike me because of who I am."

"Don't worry. You won't be put with common criminals. People accused of terror crimes are always grouped together."

What kind of people would he put me with? The prosecutor had mentioned both FETO and the PKK. If he sent me to a PKK cell, it would be a rougher crowd—men who had spent years fighting in the mountains. What would they do to me? On the plus side, I would learn to speak Kurdish . . .

"Don't worry," said the director, his face blank. "I'm putting you in with some Gulenists. They're all harmless. Most of them are just schoolteachers."

94

Minutes later I was standing outside another solid metal door, watching one of the guards pull back bolts as long as his arm and open at least three separate locks—a thick bolt with a heavy padlock, a deadbolt, and a third separate mechanism that required something like a tire-changing tool to turn it and shoot bolts into the steel frame. There was no getting out of this cell.

With great apprehension I stepped inside.

Eleven faces turned from the TV on the wall and fixed their eyes on me. They were sitting on plastic chairs around two plastic tables eating sunflower seeds.

"I have a new friend for you," said the head guard. "Someone help him find a bed." He left and the door locks clicked into place behind me.

One of the men spoke up. "Who are you?"

"Have you eaten?" said another voice. "We have cookies if you want one."

"Have some tea."

Their faces were interested, kind even. They certainly looked a lot more like teachers than terrorists.

I opened my mouth to speak, but burst out weeping. I had held in my emotions since leaving Norine, but now my defenses collapsed at their welcome.

LATER, AS I LAY ON MY BUNK—a bottom one that the youngest inmate had given me when I told him that I'd had neck surgery six months earlier—I could hear the tinkling of the tea glasses as they stirred the sugar cubes in and their talking while the TV played on. I could also smell their cigarette smoke wafting up to the sleeping area. I still felt relieved at my cellmates' reception.

But I was terrified as well. Sakran was worse than anything I had experienced so far. The locks, the bars, the way the guards behaved—it was impossible to ignore the fact that I was now in a real prison.

I was being treated like a genuine terrorist.

10 | MELTDOWN

SAKRAN MAY BE LARGE, but you'd never know it from behind your locked and bolted door. Each cell is a self-contained duplex. Bunk beds fill a sleeping area upstairs and downstairs ten people can crowd together around two small plastic tables for meals. There's a single shower, a single squat toilet, and a single door that opens onto an inner courtyard with thirty-foot-high walls crowned with razor wire. This is where prisoners wash their clothes in a bucket and hang them out to dry.

Sakran was designed to keep prisoners away from society and away from each other. So there are no communal spaces, no daily program of activities, no common dining area, and no time in any day where you can leave your cell and move around.

You're locked up 24/7. Once a week you're allowed out to make a ten-minute phone call—although for political prisoners like me it was once every two weeks. Once a week you receive a thirty-five-minute visit in person, though you're separated by thick glass and have to speak through a telephone. And once every two months you hit the jackpot: an open visit where you can finally sit in the same room as your visitor. If the bars and the crowding and the lack of sunlight don't get you, the fact that you are only allowed to hold hands with your wife six times a year is guaranteed to cut deep.

If your lawyer comes, you'll be allowed an hour each week, but every moment of your meeting will be recorded on video. Apart from that, for every minute of every day, you're trapped in your cell. You could spend year after year there and never meet a prisoner from another cell.

If you have money the prison will sell you items from their list, like plastic tables and chairs, fridges, and TVs—though naturally they control the channels that are available. You can buy extra food—like the cookies I was offered on my first night—and certain approved newspapers. Each cell has to pay for its own faucets, light bulbs, electricity, drinking water, plastic eating utensils, and plates. The prison provides the room and the locks; everything else has a price.

When it's time to deliver food, the guards come to the door in pairs and slop the meal into the communal bowls that inmates pass through the hatch in the door.

Sakran does not do rehabilitation.

What Sakran does is isolation.

MY ARRIVAL that Friday night pushed the number of occupants of the cell made for eight up to twelve. Although it was already crowded, my cellmates welcomed a new person to interact with. But I was falling apart. I didn't want to talk and I didn't want to listen to stories. I could not engage much, and yet had nothing with which to occupy myself. I had no Bible, no books, no certainty. I spent most of that first weekend on my bed crying, desperate and totally confused.

Here and there I asked questions, bit by bit learning the rules and restrictions and how awful it was.

I learned that our cell's visiting day was Monday and resolved to hold on until I could see Norine. I was sure she would be at the prison gates, figuring out how to get in to see me—and I so needed to see her.

Monday was also the day when my lawyer would appeal my imprisonment. This was a face-saving opportunity for the Turkish government—a judge could order my release while the investigation continued. After all, there was not even a case against me, just unofficial allegations.

And, Monday was the twelfth. Maybe—just maybe—God was still going to move at the last minute.

ON MONDAY the cell door opened and the guards announced that it was time for people to have their weekly visit with their family members. I stood up and filed toward the door.

"No, not you," said the guard, his arm out across my chest. "You don't have a visit."

"Why not? They're all seeing their wives, so why can't I see mine?"

"Because you're a foreigner. You have no visitation rights. Your wife can apply to Ankara for permission, and they will decide."

That was all there was to say.

The door slammed and locked.

FOR A MINUTE I was just stunned, then the panic began to build. I tried walking upstairs and sitting on my bunk, but that didn't help. Every breath left my chest feeling tighter. I wanted to run, but there was nowhere to go.

I burst out through the door downstairs into the courtyard. I paced the rectangle full of angst. Seven paces. Turn. Five paces. Turn. Seven paces. Turn. And then I stopped. I was facing the wall that towered up so far above me I could only see a tiny rectangle of sky. I was at the bottom of a pit.

Suddenly the words came up from the deepest, the darkest, the most angry part of me.

You've betrayed me! You've turned me over! Why?!

How could you do this to a son who loves you, a son who has obeyed you?

Do you even care, or have you handed me over and walked away?

Did you deceive me? Did you lie to me?

BEING THROWN IN PRISON had been such a drastic, unexpected change—it simply hadn't happened to any missionaries in Turkey, so I had never prepared myself. I couldn't cope with the horde of questions plaguing my mind. And there was no one I could go to.

Not to my cellmates who were Muslim and would not understand me at all—to them the idea that I would question God was inconceivable.

Not to the God I loved, whom I addressed as Papa. He had turned me over to be savaged.

Not even to Norine, whom I was desperate to see. I needed her to hear my terrible thoughts and to speak truth to me, to persuade me that I was wrong.

But I could only talk to myself. Or to God—I had to keep talking to him . . . and WHY was he so silent? I yelled at him, not out loud but in my heart: *I may as well talk to this wall!*

All I heard was silence.

My tears blinded me. *Where are you when I most need you? You have wounded my heart. How can I ever recover?*

I was having a faith meltdown.

All the progress I'd made in my final weeks in Harmandali—where I prayed many times a day to surrender to God's plan—had vanished.

THE GUARDS CAME to lock up the courtyard. It was 5:00 p.m.

My watch had stopped working in the early morning hours of December 12. When I saw in the night that the hands were frozen on the ten and two—which I immediately noted added up to 12—I had felt an ominous chill go through my body. The twelfth was over now. Clearly my appeal had been denied. I was still in prison.

Even my watch was mocking me.

I FOUND OUT that all my cellmates were new to Sakran. They told me they had been transferred from a freezing, decrepit prison in the mountains called Buca. According to them, Sakran was an improvement.

I also discovered that the director had only shared part of the story when he told me that they were teachers. Some of them had worked at schools run by the Gulen movement, but six of my cellmates were from the police, and two were chiefs.

In the aftermath of the attempted coup the atmosphere among the public in Turkey had been tense. Among the police and judiciary it had been frantic. Not only was Erdogan taking advantage of the opportunity to lock away political opponents, but ambitious prosecutors, judges, and members of the police were also accusing colleagues of being Gulenists in order to secure their own status. Others were doing it to save their own skins.

Someone who had been arrested would be offered a deal: tell us who has been involved with Gulen and we will let you go—*if* you give enough names. Some desperate men would list all their colleagues, who would then be rounded up and thrown into prison. No evidence was necessary—being on someone's list was enough.

One of my cellmates had been accused of attending a picnic with Gulenists ten years ago—at a time when Erdogan himself was praising Gulen. We had even heard that the former director of Sakran was now a prisoner in his own prison. One day you could be doing your job, arresting suspects and helping track down the plotters, while the next day a secret witness could accuse you of being disloyal, without submitting any evidence, and you'd be hauled up before a judge.

This is what happened to another of my cellmates. He had been taken before a judge he knew well, begged for his freedom, and protested his innocence. "I know," said the judge. "But it's either you or me. If I don't send you to prison they'll send me there instead."

One by one I heard stories just like this. Some of the men knew the identity of the colleague who had deliberately stabbed them in the back, while others could only guess.

One of them, a man in his midthirties called Emin, stood out. His family was wealthy and well known throughout Turkey. His father knew Erdogan but was accused of employing Gulenist teachers in the university he'd established. They'd arrested the father first, then had gone after Emin, accusing him of taking money to Kazakstan to fund Gulenist schools there.

Emin smiled when he told me how the prosecutor had listed the dates that he'd believed Emin was in Kazakstan. "I showed them my passport, proving that I was not out of the country when they said I was, but they locked me up anyway. Okan Batu had decided to go after my family."

"Okan Batu?" I said, remembering the wolfish prosecutor who'd stared at me with such hatred in the courthouse.

The cell hummed with murmurs of disgust, but there was little surprise in their voices. I stayed silent. I had had a lot of time to think about my case. As a first step, some official in Ankara made a decision to deport us. But then someone, somewhere, at a higher level, made a choice: "Let's keep him and see how we can use this." I was an American, a Christian, and a missionary—three categories that combined to make me an attractive target. That's how I ended up in Harmandali. They also wanted to make an example of me in order to intimidate other missionaries.

But now what was being done to me had reached a much higher level. It was Okan Batu who demanded I be sent to prison. But thanks to Senator Corker I knew my case had gone to the top of the Turkish government. Just days before my arrest seventeen senators had asked Erdogan for my release. Sending me to Sakran was his response.

EVEN THOUGH OKAN BATU was not ultimately the man keeping me in prison, this did not keep him from harassing me in a dream.

The sleep troubles that had worn me down at Harmandali continued in Sakran. When I was finally able to fall asleep I was frequently tormented by terrible nightmares where I was surrounded by an evil darkness. One night, creeping out from the shadows, I saw Okan Batu approach me. He climbed onto my chest and pressed down on me with all his might. "We're going to keep you here for months," he said, his wolfish eyes piercing mine. "And then we're going to convict you." Even when I slept I couldn't rest. I was exhausted all the time.

I HAD NOTHING TO CHANGE INTO. I had been wearing the same smelly clothes for days—since I was taken from Harmandali. Maybe somebody noticed, because the same young man who had traded bunks with me loaned me a pair of sweats and a T-shirt. Another cellmate gave me a towel—and within a few days I had developed a nasty yeast infection on my inner thighs that became raw. I could barely walk, and I wrote to Norine, "Now I really have become Job."

I had written a letter to Norine every day since I arrived in Sakran, pouring out my heart. I was only allowed to write in Turkish, which just didn't feel the same. Still it helped me to know that Norine would eventually be able to read about my struggles, and respond.

I needed to hear from Norine. I was desperate to find out what was happening on the outside—was anything being done? And was she okay—was she even still in the country? As I wrote our address on the envelope, I sometimes feared that I was writing to an empty home.

One day a guard opened the hatch in the metal door and called my name.

The hatch was set low, about waist height, so the only way for me to see the person on the other side was to kneel and crane my neck. As I looked up at the guard, I saw he was holding a piece of paper. "We're not sending your letters on. We deem them to be a threat to the security of the prison so we're confiscating them."

I was stunned. "What's going on?"

"You wrote to your wife and talked about 'the Lord' and how you wanted his help. You're obviously referring to Fethullah Gulen. You're sending secret messages."

"No," I said, trying to sound calm. "I'm not talking about Gulen. I'm writing about God."

He passed me the piece of paper. "Sign this. The prison has opened a court case against you because of your letters." As soon as I handed the paper back, the hatch slammed shut. Discussion over.

This was absurd. But they were serious.

Over the coming days I learned how cut off I was. I needed to tell my lawyer, but I was not allowed to call her, and the prison would not contact her either. I could write a letter, and hope it would be sent sometime soon. But in the meantime, my case would go ahead, with or without a defense.

I became anxious as I waited for news from the court. On the first day the prison had given me a sheet with a list of punishments. The prison could cut me off from all contact, like visits, for months. They could throw me into solitary confinement. As much as the cell was uncomfortable, crowded, and noisy, it was better than the torture of being alone.

The first judge who reviewed the case involving my letters said, "This man is obviously writing love letters to his wife," and threw it out. The prison director appealed to a higher court who reversed the decision, claiming that my comments to Norine were in fact a threat to the security of the prison, and that I was a bad example to other prisoners. From then on, any letters I wrote were examined by the prosecutor's office. It was the same with any letters she sent to me.

MY LETTERS weren't the only source of controversy. On the Monday after my first weekend in Sakran I was accused of trying to smuggle a flash drive into the prison. They had found a USB stick in my backpack when they finally processed my belongings. The stick had been in my backpack since going to the police station on October 7. But in any case, I had not touched my backpack since arriving at the prison—it had been in their possession the whole time. So how could I have smuggled it in? But they still opened a case against me, and then said there was evidence hidden on the drive.

It seemed they were trying to concoct excuses to punish me. I had done nothing, I was innocent, and they kept accusing me of things that could lead to even worse conditions in prison. And I questioned God: *At Harmandali you showed kindness in providing some things for me in the presence of my enemies. Now each of them has been taken away. And every decision in prison is against me—it keeps getting worse and worse. Where are you in all of this?!*

I felt completely abandoned.

TWO DAYS BEFORE CHRISTMAS I received my first piece of mail. It was our most recent family picture, taken a year ago at Christmas.

Norine had sent it on its own, without any writing, in hopes that it would get through more easily. I wept inconsolably.

I would not be home for Christmas.

THE DAY AFTER CHRISTMAS was an open visit. Everyone would get to be in the same room with their family. But not me.

By now I had gone almost three weeks without seeing Norine. I was cut off, and I was growing increasingly desperate. My letters had been confiscated, no letters were getting through to me, and I was not allowed to make the phone call the other men had every two weeks. I was isolated by my culture, life experience, nationality, and most importantly by my faith. The prison had opened two new court cases against me, and I knew that this government was set against me at the highest levels. I was overwhelmed with the sense of spiritual darkness.

And two fears were pushing me toward the edge.

I was afraid I was going insane. Emin had loaned me a Sherlock Holmes novel in Turkish. I read a chapter, and when I lay the book down I had such a surreal sense, a sense of dislocation—*Where am I? Is this real?*

My dreams seemed so real. Then I would wake to a real-life nightmare, disoriented at first, but then realizing where I was when the bars in the window came into focus. There were times when I could feel myself tipping over into insanity, and I had to make an effort to pull myself back to the other side. I tasted insanity, and I was afraid I would go there and not come back.

Even more terrifying was the fear that I might lose my faith. I had no desire to reject my faith—actually, I was desperately clinging to it. But I was afraid that with all my questions, doubts, and isolation from anyone who could encourage and correct me, I would in some way fail and turn away. The words of Jesus came to mind—that if your hand causes you to sin, then it's better to cut off the hand and go to heaven than to keep both but go to hell. Wouldn't it be better to kill myself to ensure that I didn't lose my faith? In my twisted thinking it made sense.

WHEN THE MEN FILED OUT to meet their families on December 26, I was the only one left behind in the cell. I went out to the court-yard. I tested the rope. Yes, the clothesline was strong enough to hold my weight.

I was ready to go to heaven.

11 | THE CRUELEST WHISPER

IT GAVE ME A SENSE OF COMFORT to know that I could escape this nightmare. And knowing this lifted my despair just enough to help me hold on.

Two days after I tested the rope I was back in the courtyard, pacing as usual, when my cellmates started shouting my name. "You've got a visitor! It's your wife!"

Three weeks had passed since I'd arrived in Sakran and I'd been thinking about Norine nonstop. I'd been wondering how long it would take before she was allowed to see me. To know that she had finally made it to Sakran and that she was here to see me right now left me almost euphoric. I ran up to my bunk, grabbed my toothbrush, and headed to the bathroom.

"What are you doing?" said Emin. "They're taking it off your time already. Just go!"

AS SOON AS I WAS SHOWN into the room where Norine was waiting, I broke down. It wasn't just Norine who had been allowed to visit, but my mother too. The guard had told me as we'd walked from the cell that this was an open visit, which meant that I would be allowed to talk in English. But for the first five minutes all I could do was sob.

"Hey, my love," said Norine as she rocked me gently in her arms. "It's okay. I'm here. I found you, right?"

With three guards looking on, we sat side by side at a table in a corner of the room. Norine and I clung to each other the entire visit.

When I finally could speak, I was desperate to explain the spiritual crisis that was suffocating me. "Norine, I am Job," I said. "I am Job. God has turned me over to Satan." I was unshaven, distraught, and unraveling.

My mother was concerned that I was heading down a dangerous path by blaming God. "You know, Andrew, I made a mistake in telling you at Harmandali that you were God's prisoner. Actually, you are a prisoner *for* God." I knew what she was doing, trying to give me a right perspective, but I wasn't ready to write this off completely to persecution. I was convinced that God had planned to set me free but changed his mind to accomplish some purpose—what exactly, I did not know. And this meant that ultimately he was the one keeping me in prison. In the end, he was my jailor.

Norine explained how she had been trying to get to me since day one, even coming out the very first Saturday. But there was no bend in this place. To come in today they'd been through multiple security checks, a thorough search, and had had their irises scanned twice. Mom had not even been allowed to keep a Kleenex with her. The high walls, the security, the iron bars—it was imposing and intimidating.

"I hope we can finally have a phone call this week. Because our home phone and my cell phone were registered in your name, the prison would not approve those numbers. I had to get a new number and register it in my name and then mail all the paperwork in. I've been working on it."

I was sure she had been. I knew that Norine would keep fighting for me.

But I knew that we were both powerless here.

MY NIGHTMARE about Okan Batu had been troubling me, but there was another dream that I wanted to tell Norine about.

It was one of those dreams where you sense rather than see something happening, and in mine I was aware that Turkey, Iran, and Russia were coming together to form an alliance so dark that I woke up sweating and gasping for breath. It seemed counterintuitive, as Turkey and Iran were historical enemies. As for Russia, Turkey had shot down one of its jets a year earlier and the two countries were on opposite sides of the conflict in Syria. Then, three days after my dream, an off-duty Turkish police officer assassinated the Russian ambassador at an art exhibition in Ankara. I thought it would drive them apart, but as the story dominated the news in the coming days it became clear that the incident had brought Erdogan and Putin closer together.

The dream scared me. "Norine, you've got to get me out of here before this happens."

I wanted her to understand the urgency I felt. If Turkey turned away from its Western alliances toward what I had seen, it would be bad news—and very bad news for me.

"Time's up," said one of the guards.

"Is it going to be another three weeks until I see you again?" I said in a pained voice.

Norine's voice was soft. "I don't know when I'm going to see you again."

I understood.

They had done everything they could to encourage me in this short time, but I needed something to hold on to, a sliver of hope, no matter how vague and insubstantial. I asked the one question that had been growing within me ever since I'd arrived. "Am I going to grow old and die in this place?"

I could hear Norine's breath catch in her throat.

A FEW DAYS LATER, on my forty-ninth birthday, things in the cell got worse.

The door opened in the afternoon and a man came in carrying a couple of trash bags full of his possessions. A few minutes later the door opened again, delivering another inmate. Another came after that, and by the end of the day we had gone from twelve to eighteen men in a cell built for eight. Even though many criminals had actually been released to make space for the FETO prisoners, there still wasn't enough room for the huge numbers arrested. And new prisons couldn't be built fast enough.

The bunk beds filled up, and the last four to arrive were given a mattress and told to find a space to sleep on the floor. The two-foot gap between my bunk and my neighbor's became home to a military policeman in his twenties. Right from the beginning it was clear that he tolerated but did not like me, which added to my stress. When we were each in our beds we would often end up with our faces just inches apart.

I was glad to have a bed—it was the only place I could retreat to. Every afternoon I would pull out paper and write a letter to Norine, pouring out my anxieties. I wrote the same things again and again: "Am I a Peter, or a James?" They were two of Jesus's closest disciples: Peter was released from prison, James was not.

In the same way that I kept asking the same questions, I also needed to hear the same reassurances again and again from Norine.

One of the most painful worries I had was about her. And my dreams didn't help. In many of them I was with Norine, but then she would disappear, or she would be in a place where I could see her but not reach her. She sometimes seemed not to care. And when I woke up, the feelings of her being distant or leaving me behind would still be there. I had to repeat to myself: *This is only a dream! This is not really Norine!*

I knew that she would remain faithful, but I wondered whether she was going to go back to normal life. Sundays were especially difficult. It had been the highlight of my week for so many years, and it was the one day when I knew where she'd be and what she'd be doing at any given hour. I knew when she'd be leaving the apartment, when our church service would be starting, and when it would finish. I'd picture everyone going out for a meal after the meeting, just like I had done with them so many times. Was she with them? Was she moving on, having fun, enjoying life?

In all our life together Norine had never given me reason to doubt her. On her lowest day, when she was released from Isikkent, she fought to stay with me. I knew she loved me; I'd always known it. And even in the cell I knew that my fears were baseless, but I felt them all the same. She's my closest confidant, the person in the world I most desire to be with. I have never spent too much time with her. I have never needed time away from her. We did everything together.

So the whisper that came in the darkest moments—that Norine wasn't missing me, that she had moved on or would move on and eventually forget me—that was the cruelest whisper of all. I knew it was irrational, but it was demoralizing.

When we were finally allowed a phone call and I told her about my fears, she said exactly what I needed to hear.

"Andrew, I cannot have a normal life without you, and I don't want to. Would you feel any differently if our positions were reversed? It's my honor to be walking through this with you. My love, I'm waiting for you. We will go back to normal life *together*."

I was comforted. It sounds pathetic now, but I said, "I need to hear this often. Keep telling me."

Then I asked her the biggest question of all. "Do you have hope? Will I get out of here?"

Even before she said a word I felt as though my insides had been crushed by a vice. The silence only lasted a second or two, but I could tell she was weighing her words carefully.

"I don't know," she said softly. "I'm not God."

The panic was fiercer than ever. It was like I was clawing the walls. "You've got to get me out of here, Norine. You've got to get me out."

"Calm down, my love."

The phone died. We had reached our ten-minute mark. I followed the guards back to the cell. I said nothing as I picked my way through the crowd and out into the cold air of the courtyard.

I was devastated. I was barely holding on. If Norine didn't have hope that I'd get out, then I might as well give up.

I remembered the stories I'd heard over the years of Chinese Christians persecuted by the state. In every tale where they were locked up inside brutal prisons, they seemed to be so joyful. They were suffering for their faith, yet somehow they made persecution look like a privilege. It was inspiring. I wanted to be like them. But I wasn't.

How could I be so broken by prison? What was wrong with me? I said time and again, "God, you chose the wrong man." Why would he put me in a place where I would start to believe that it's harder to live for God than it is to die for him?

ON JANUARY 20, 2017, I was given another reminder of how far everything was slipping away from me. For once I was watching the TV in the cell. It was showing some US news, the inauguration of President Donald Trump.

Norine had spent weeks trying to get through to someone in the President-elect's team, and our best hope so far was Franklin Graham. He grew up in the same church back in North Carolina that my family attended. Amazingly, Franklin had been invited to take part in the ceremony, and we'd heard that he was going to raise my case with Trump if he could.

I watched in silence.

Franklin was right there, in front of the microphone. He was praying, and President Trump was right there too. He was so close, and I was pleading with God to let the two men talk.

After that, days slipped by.

Nothing changed.

LIFE IN T4 C BLOCK continued—excruciatingly slowly.

Erol was the first to go on trial from our cell. This was a big deal, because everyone else had been held for months now, with no movement on their cases—no indictments, no trial dates, and no end in sight. Erol was a quiet and gentle man who worked for the forestry department. When his wife brought their four-year-old to the open visits, she would tell the boy that his father was working in this building. She asked one of the guards to play along. "Dad works here, right?" It was very sad.

Erol had been arrested for a simple reason: he had an app on his phone.

ByLock was a secure messaging app that had been freely available. The problem for Erol was that some of the people who planned the coup had used ByLock to communicate. When the government discovered this, it cracked the server and started arresting anyone who had used it.

The day Erol went to court for his third trial appearance, the cell was tense, even though everyone agreed that the ByLock charges were absurd. Before Erol left the cell, one of the former police chiefs laid out exactly why he was going to come back a free man. "There's no criminality proven, and no connection to the coup plotters. It is simply not possible to convict you—the courts will not allow it."

His words made sense, they sounded logical. But this was Turkey in the aftermath of the coup. Logic didn't count for much.

Erol left, nervous but looking cautiously optimistic. The rest of the men spent much of the day talking nervously and doing their prayers. They discussed their cases and I found out that at least six others in the cell had also been caught with ByLock on their phones. Someone else had been arrested for having an account at Asya Bank, a bank linked to the Gulenist movement. Just having an account there was enough to land someone in Sakran, even though when the first branch was opened, none other than Erdogan himself had held the ribbon as it was cut.

As time passed, I listened to my cellmates' conversation settle on a new topic.

"When I get out of here they're going to owe me so much money in compensation."

"Oh yeah. Seven hundred dollars per month!"

"Plus you can sue for missed earnings and damages."

"I heard about a guy who got $100,000. Can you believe it?"

"I'm buying myself a summer cottage."

"Hey, Andrew. You can really sue. An American locked away for months like this? They're going to owe you big-time!"

I just smiled and nodded.

There was no way that any of them were going to be able to sue.

As the evening arrived, the sense of anticipation about Erol's return increased.

As soon as he walked in, the atmosphere changed.

Erol sat at the table, his face drained of color, his voice shaky and weak. "I pleaded with the judge to look at my messages and see that they were just the kind of normal things you send to your family and friends. There was nothing to do with the coup in there. Nothing to do with anything. But the judge said that just having the app meant that I was part of FETO. Then he gave me ten years."

We all sat in silence.

It wasn't just the others who had ByLock on their phones who took it hard. All of us did. We all knew then that there was nothing about this judicial system that was fair or independent.

There was no way out.

12 | THE MOUTH OF HELL

WHEN YOU'RE LOCKED UP IN A COUNTRY whose legal systems are corrupt and judicial independence is a myth, you're at the mercy of people with far more power than you. One of your only hopes is that someone, somewhere can use their influence to help you.

Not long after I'd been taken to Sakran, some friends put Norine in contact with Mustafa, a Turkish businessman who offered to help. He explained that his lawyer knew both my prosecutor and the judge who had sent me to the prison, and he felt very confident that working with his lawyer he could get the case dismissed and me on a plane home. All we needed to do was pay $35,000 to cover the lawyer's fees.

It was a lot of money—money that we didn't have in our bank account but would have to borrow from friends and family. Norine did her research. Mustafa knew people in the US and he'd been attending the National Prayer Breakfast for years. If he was operating at the level he said he was, then it seemed to Norine that he wouldn't want to damage his relationships in the US over what had to be a small amount to him.

So she decided to do it. She could only get together $25,000. Norine wired it, but within a few days she grew uneasy. Mustafa claimed that the money hadn't arrived. When she put in an official request for the wire to be recalled, the bank replied that the money had been deposited and the account owner refused to return the funds. Mustafa had scammed us.

I knew from Emin that this kind of thing was happening to others, as unscrupulous people took advantage of others in distress. This was back when Norine's requests for visits were not being approved, so she had to make the decision on her own. I was not upset so much about the loss—I was angry at the person who manipulated and cheated my wife. But she was doing everything she could to get me out. This payment was out of love for me.

MY VISITS WITH NORINE became more frequent. I couldn't know ahead of time if she had received permission, so I would wait anxiously near the door as the guard called out through the slot the names for the first group. If my name wasn't called, I'd wait for the second group and hope. Although fifty minutes were allotted for each cell, coming and going to the visiting area shaved off fifteen minutes. The door would clang open and the first group of ten prisoners would walk out and line up in single file. After taking our shoes off we would be frisked and then follow a guard in single file through several security doors. I would lunge for the cubicle where Norine was waiting and place my hand opposite hers—separated by thick glass—and Norine would pray for me. "I bless you in the name of the Lord. I speak hope to you."

She would ask God ahead of time for something to pray and speak over me each week, and then literally lift her head high as she approached the prison gate with a deliberate mindset: *I am a daughter of the King, and I am here to see a son of the King.*

I was afraid of being forgotten. I also worried that people would stop praying, move on to the next crisis, but every week Norine told me news of new places. "Iranians are praying. In China a million brochures were printed about you. The German Evangelical Alliance just had a day of fasting and prayer for you. Christians in Spain, Korea, Madagascar, Hungary, Mexico, and Lebanon are praying. I can't keep track of all the countries. Our friend Leyla has been skipping all desserts on Sundays and you know how much she loves sweets. And David is continuing to fast from coffee until you are released."

I did not feel worthy of all this prayer. How could Chinese and Iranians be praying for me when they had so many of their own in prison? I knew brothers and sisters I had never met were fighting for me, and I was deeply grateful for it.

ENCOURAGEMENT ON THE DIPLOMATIC FRONT came soon. We had been hoping that the new administration would actively work on our behalf. In February Norine heard that Vice President Mike Pence and Secretary of State Rex Tillerson both talked with their Turkish counterparts about me. Seventy-eight senators and members of Congress had joined the bipartisan effort to urge Ankara to release me. Knowing that people at the highest levels were now advocating for me was a significant boost.

The question was whether Turkey would respond well. When Secretary of State John Kerry had talked about me to his Turkish counterpart he was rebuffed, and when a senator raised my case with the Turkish ambassador to the US, he had turned his back on him and walked away without a word. This hard attitude had been evident even in the way our consular officials were treated when they visited me at Sakran.

ANOTHER ANSWER TO PRAYER came in a more roundabout way. Somebody who knew somebody who knew somebody reached an aide to the Turkish prime minister. One day Norine received a phone call from Adnan Bey, one of the prison directors.

"When is your next visit with your husband? You can bring some books." He had acted very dismissively before, so this was a change.

First it was only Turkish books, but within a short time English books were allowed as well. This was a lifesaver—a Bible, Christian books, novels, some history. Now I had something that helped me fill the long hours. I told Norine that one day in prison was like ten outside—they went by so very slowly. And it was a great comfort to have a Bible, even just to hold it in my hands.

MY NEW ROUTINE now included walking as soon as the courtyard was unlocked in the morning, trying to nap in the afternoon, and letter writing and reading at night. One afternoon I had an unusual dream. I saw my name written on a sheet of paper. Next to my name was the number sixty-eight. In the dream itself I suddenly understood that this was the number of days until my release. Then I woke up. I counted forward. *Sixty-eight days takes me to May 22. Could this be possible?* I let it sit in the back of my mind.

In all my hurt and disappointment, I had not stopped talking to God. I had accused him of deceiving me, but I had asked forgiveness. Every day I spent hours and hours talking to God—when I paced outside in the courtyard, when I lay on my bed trying to pass the time, at night when I tried to go to sleep, when I woke throughout the night. And I began to think that God was talking back.

Because I really needed Norine to be with me in Turkey she could not campaign for my release in person in the States. But when she heard that Rex Tillerson, the new secretary of state, was coming to Ankara and would talk with President Erdogan, she tried very hard to get a meeting with him. That week I kept asking God to arrange this for Norine. Several times the thought came to me: *He will meet with Norine. Because you are on my agenda, I will put you on his agenda.* When I saw her at our next Monday visit, I told her what I thought I was hearing. Norine had asked for a meeting through Senator James Lankford and Phil Kosnett, the chargé d'affaires at the embassy, but on Tuesday both came back with the same answer: there will be no meeting. She was told there was no point in going to Ankara.

But Norine went anyway, because of what I had told her. She waited. Back at Sakran I was lying on my bed, praying, begging God to come through with this meeting. If it did not happen, it meant that I really was not hearing from God. At 4:00 p.m. the thought flashed in my mind, *It's done.* What? What's done? Had Tillerson left? Is it all over? The next day my lawyer brought word from Norine. At 4:00 p.m. she had received a call telling her to come meet Tillerson at his hotel.

God had put me on Tillerson's agenda. *He was speaking to me!*

NORINE MET WITH SECRETARY TILLERSON on a Thursday, and I met with my lawyer, Suna, on Friday. She and Norine had stopped by the prosecutor's office that morning and for the first time ever, Suna looked upbeat. She was even smiling.

"Secretary Tillerson brought you up with President Erdogan, who said he was aware of your case. And—listen to this, Andrew—Erdogan told Tillerson that an indictment is about to be handed down. The prosecutor said that he is wrapping everything up in the next two weeks. He is telling the police they have one week to submit whatever evidence they have gathered, and whatever they don't have, too bad, it'll be too late. He said he would then evaluate whatever the police presented. If there is nothing there, he will drop the case, and you will be released."

I let her words settle, drinking them in. For the first time in months I could feel hope rise inside of me.

A COUPLE OF WEEKS PASSED. Nothing happened. Norine went back to the prosecutor, but he was evasive.

Suna returned to see me. She was no longer smiling.

"I don't want you to get your hopes up anymore, Andrew."

"You don't have to worry about that, Suna."

"The prosecutor has been walking it back, saying that there's a video of you that's evidence."

"What video? Evidence of what?"

"I don't know. Your files are sealed."

I was frustrated. And I was worried too. Something had changed at the top again, and I was fairly sure there was a political calculation in keeping me. Turkey was about to hold a referendum on Erdogan, switching to a presidential system that would give him by law the power that he had already taken in practice. At best, my case would be on hold while the referendum took place.

FOLLOWING ERDOGAN'S TRIUMPH in the April referendum, President Trump invited him to come to Washington for a summit on May 16. The news from the presummit meetings was good. Based on information she was receiving, CeCe, our attorney at the ACLJ, had even suggested to Norine that a June wedding for our daughter Jacqueline looked possible. I could be walking her down the aisle soon.

I was still anxious, but when Norine told me that I'd been put on the agenda for the summit—that Presidents Trump and Erdogan themselves would be talking about me—I let myself begin to hope.

Surely this would do it. It would cost Erdogan nothing to release me as a gesture of goodwill, since he knew that I was innocent.

Between the news of the summit and the memory of my dream that pointed to May 22 as the date of my release, I took a step of faith. I was not sure, I was very anxious, but I sent home my winter clothes and packed my belongings, dividing up what I would take from what I would leave behind in prison.

THE SIGNS WERE GOOD, but a couple of things that highlighted the cynicism of the Turkish government made me uneasy.

On the weekend of May 1—a holiday weekend—the prosecutor asked Norine for the passcode to my phone. They had taken my phone on October 7, and now, eight months later, had finally decided to examine it. They were fishing for something—anything—before they went to the US. And in the presummit meetings Mevlut Cavusoglu, the foreign minister, had told the US delegation, "We were going to let Brunson go two weeks ago, but he said he wanted to stay." This was absurd. I had written numerous times asking to return to the US. My lawyer rushed to have me sign a statement saying that I expressly wanted to leave Turkey. But there had been enough bumps in the road already to know that no exit was going to be smooth.

THE DAY OF THE SUMMIT my cellmates were glued to the TV as events in Washington were covered. I couldn't watch. I spent the day fasting and praying desperately. That night I could hear the commentary as President Erdogan shook hands with President Trump in the Oval Office. The summit began.

It lasted all of twenty-three minutes.

I lay on my bunk and wept. How could I have been brought up if they had so little time together? Everything told me that whatever opportunity there had been for me to be released had just been dashed.

I SPENT THE NEXT MORNING pacing in the courtyard, hoping that somehow there had been a conversation about me between the two leaders.

A few hours in it happened. Some of my cellmates started yelling my name. "Get in here, Andrew. They're talking about you on TV!"

The commentators were telling how President Trump hadn't just brought me up once, but had asked for me three times during their short conversation.

"This is really astounding," said one. "All the big issues they have to discuss and this is the thing that Trump chooses to bring up three times? Who is this priest, anyway?" The other news channels were telling the same story.

Some of my cellmates congratulated me. "Andrew, your president asked for you. It won't be long now. Maybe tomorrow, or at most a few weeks while they find a way to let you go without losing face."

I wasn't just astounded. I was delighted. It was one thing for President Trump to bring me up at all in such a short meeting. But three times? I couldn't have asked for more.

Months ago I had mused to Norine, "If two presidents end up talking about me, it will be a miracle." It is very difficult to get to the US president. And if you can get to him, will he show interest? And if he shows interest, will he remember later? And if he does remember, will he do anything about it? They had talked about me. Here was my miracle. For a few moments I let myself wonder how long it would take before I was home.

But one news host had a different take. He made his own suggestion for how to deal with me.

"You know what I would say if I were writing a newspaper headline? I'd say, 'Give us the Imam and take the priest.'"

I could feel the ground starting to slip beneath my feet. The Imam was Fethullah Gulen, enemy number one in Turkey, and the man Erdogan was blaming for masterminding the failed coup attempt. He was living in Pennsylvania, and Erdogan wanted him sent back.

THE NEXT DAY I was in the courtyard pacing when I heard a yell. "Andrew, you are on TV again."

The foreign minister was talking about me on a national news channel. He didn't just look serious, he looked angry. "The priest Brunson is a terrorist," Cavusoglu spat. "He is linked to FETO. He is also linked to the PKK. We have given his file to the Americans with all the evidence against him. This case will continue as a judicial matter."

I was crushed. One of the top government officials—Erdogan's messenger—was publicly declaring that I was guilty of being a terrorist. No court in Turkey would ever let me go now.

A few hours later the newspapers were delivered. I didn't want to look, but I knew I had to. One headline covered the entire front page: *Give Us the Imam—Take the Priest.*

The mouth of hell had opened.

PART FOUR

13 | THE SHARK

FOR DAYS THE MEDIA FEASTED ON MY STORY, accusing me of being a terrorist and calling me "Spy Priest." It was as if they were starving wolves and I was an injured lamb.

What really scared me was knowing that the government was orchestrating this onslaught. They had pointed the media in the direction they wanted them to go, and set the wolves loose. Later on I heard from someone who had actually been at the summit when President Trump asked for me. "I was watching Erdogan and I saw his face change when the president asked for your return. I was looking at him—his face changed! He had just calculated that he could leverage you for more." So this was his answer to Trump. I was devastated.

The media dug up the story about the time the gunman had marched toward our church and tried to shoot me. They announced that I was able to defeat my attacker by relying on what they ridiculously alleged was my advanced CIA training, and started calling me "Rambo Priest." Another report declared that police had raided our apartment—they hadn't—and found a stash of special forces training manuals proving that I was a US military officer secretly commanding many other US special forces in Turkey.

As the story dragged on the claims grew wilder. I was accused of helping to organize the attempted coup, then of being the CIA's agent in charge of Turkey, and even the whole Middle East region. And others reported as fact that I had even been offered the job of director of the CIA if I had successfully brought down Erdogan in the coup.

I could almost have found it funny except that they were deadly serious, and this sent fear swarming all over me. Each morning, as soon as the guards opened the door to the courtyard, I was outside, pacing the seven steps by five steps over and over again. I wanted to tire myself out, hoping that if I walked enough during the day I'd then stand a chance of getting some sleep at night. I was desperate to sleep.

It was more than a choice, though. I was unable to stay still for even the shortest time. I had to keep moving, because whenever I tried to sit panic would start to rise within me and I'd find myself on the edge, ready to attack the walls to claw my way out. I walked constantly, and in all the months I was in Sakran I only sat down to eat a dozen times. I was like a shark: constantly alert, constantly on the move. It was the only way I could survive.

In spite of the hardline response from Erdogan, I clung to a sliver of hope that something still *could* happen. May 22, the sixty-eighth day I had seen in my dream back in March, was still a few days away. The next night, I had a dream in which I heard a beautiful song with an intricate arrangement and layers of voices unlike anything I had ever heard before—as though a choir of angels were singing. The music pulled me in, so that as I surfaced from sleep I found that I was singing the chorus—*Haleluya, the chains have been broken, haleluya*. This was clearly from God. I couldn't have made this up—in fact it was the very opposite of what I was thinking after this vile media sliming: that I would be in chains forever. In contrast this was liquid hope flowing down from heaven. Surely God was reassuring me.

ON THE MORNING OF MAY 22, my friend Kaya told me he had just dreamed that I was going to be released, and that it would happen quickly. This was supposed to be my day of deliverance, but when I saw Norine at our visit a few hours later there was nothing to celebrate. She tried to encourage me not to give up yet—something could be going on behind the scenes, and we should give it a week or two. But I was starting to break.

I knew that I would much rather be in heaven than hang on for years in a Turkish prison with the terrible isolation and oppressive spiritual environment. I was willing to force the issue.

"Norine," I said, my eyes feeling almost too heavy to keep open, "I want to go on a hunger strike if something hasn't happened by early June."

I had thought this through. It wouldn't be as immediate and irreversible as a rope, so it would give time for something to happen. And if nothing changed, then I was ready to go.

Norine looked at me. Shaking her head she said, "Don't, my love. Please wait."

Soon after I saw Norine and told her of my proposed plan I asked to see the prison doctor. I'd been aware that I'd lost weight since the previous October and wanted to know what kind of shape I was in before I started out on a hunger strike. But as I stood on the scales and saw the dial settle, I was shocked. I'd lost fifty pounds since the arrest. If I stopped eating altogether I probably wouldn't last a month, and that might not be enough time for diplomacy to work.

It sobered me up.

But it didn't change my outlook. In fact, it left me feeling even worse. Yet another way out was closed to me.

AFTER HARMANDALI I had crashed so badly. I felt betrayed, felt that God had allowed me to be deceived about expecting to get out on December 12. Over the last few months I had slowly crawled out of that pit. I thought I was hearing God speak—that I would not be here during Ramadan, the month of fasting, and that I would be home in the summer for Jacqueline's wedding. And the dream about the sixty-eight days—was that not from God? Why was God allowing me to be deceived like this—again? I could feel it all slipping away. I felt like I was in a slow-motion crash.

But the roller coaster was not over. After she'd left me on May 22, Norine received a phone call telling her that an agreement had actually been reached and the presidents were going to shake on it at a NATO summit in a few days' time. "Get your bags ready," she was told the next day. "And make sure you have some clothes packed for Andrew."

I was astounded when she told me all this. I hadn't been deceived. *My dream had been right.* Who else but God could have done this? Who else could arrange events so that precisely on the day predicted—sixty-eight days later—two governments would move?

But two days later, the Turks broke the agreement. The deal was off.

ALL MY LIFE I'd believed that God was all-powerful, that if he so much as lifted his finger in command the universe would flip. I still believed it. But the only thing I could think was that somehow God had been thwarted. He had planned to get me out—hadn't he orchestrated everything so that there was an agreement, hadn't he given me signs?—but for some reason at the last minute he just couldn't get it done. The only conclusion I could come to in that moment was that God had limited himself, that there was only so far he would go, and because of this his plan had been defeated. Either that, or he had changed his mind. Which was worse—that he changed his mind, or that he was thwarted? Both of these possibilities terrified me.

I did not even want to think about the implications. But I could not escape them. If God had decided to leave me here, or could not rescue me, then what hope did I have of ever getting out? I found myself plunged into the greatest crisis of faith and doubt that I had experienced in my life. I wasn't angry at God. I wasn't shouting at him like I had in December. I was stunned, I was dazed. I was broken—thoroughly broken.

And I was back to thinking about the rope. Although I knew it would be a shameful defeat, and I knew it was not at all what God wanted for me, I couldn't escape thoughts of suicide. Lying on my bed one day I whimpered in half-hearted defiance, "God, I don't care about my reputation. And you can worry about your own. After all, you're the one keeping me here in prison."

I was free-falling. And heaven was only a rope's length away.

I SAT OPPOSITE NORINE, separated by reinforced glass, and listened to her as she tried to encourage me.

"Promise me that you're not going to hurt yourself this week, my love. I need you to promise me that."

I leaned my head against the glass, my hand pressed up opposite hers. I was so weary in every way.

"Andrew, I speak LIFE over you. You're going to live, and not die. Our kids need a father!" She continued, "Andrew, there are so many people—so many kids praying for you. God is putting you on their hearts. They're constantly reminding their parents to pray. They won't eat until they've prayed for you. I've just heard about a little autistic boy who never forgets you. Some of them have fasted from candy or electronics. Do you know how faithful kids' prayers are and how full of faith they are? This isn't the first consideration, but it would really be a blow to all these people if you did something to yourself."

I heard her. And I promised not to hurt myself that week.

WHEN THE VISIT WAS OVER I asked the guards to take me straight to the prison director. They sat me in a chair in front of his desk. I broke down, sobbing into my hands, my body shivering violently. "I can't handle it," I said. "I have constant panic, I don't sleep. I have lost fifty pounds. I have fought for eight months to control myself, and I can't go on anymore. I need help—I need medication."

Back when I first arrived in Sakran I would have been terrified that the director would see me as a problem and remove me from the cell and put me in solitary. But anxiety had changed me. For months stress had flooded my body with adrenaline. By now it had gone on so long that my system was worn down. Panic attacks rolled in like waves. It was not just in my mind, a matter of disciplining my thoughts. No trigger was necessary. I didn't choose panic—it crashed over me. And panic mixed with despair is a deadly combination. This is why I couldn't trust myself any longer.

The prison director leaned toward me and managed a half smile. "Okay. We'll get you to a psychiatrist."

I wasn't done. "It's so hot in the cell that I can't sleep and I'm always covered in sweat. My body is worn down—I'm having a breakdown. Can I please have a fan by my bed?"

I had tried to buy a fan from the prison store before—it was on their list, so it should have been possible—but my requests had been ignored. The director told a guard, "Look in the storage area—find a fan and an extension cord and make sure it gets to him."

That afternoon the fan arrived.

This provided some immediate relief. I set it up on my bed and kept it blowing straight on me. Turks are notoriously afraid of catching cold from any draft, and some of the men in the cell started to complain that the fan was going to make them all ill. I tried to adjust its positioning according to who complained, and was relieved when the ones closest to my bed began to ask that I turn it toward them. The heat had defeated their initial misgivings.

The usual waiting time to get an appointment with a psychiatrist was a couple of months—she came to the prison once a week, and there were around ten thousand prisoners. The director must have been worried about me, because he put me on the list for an immediate visit. But the psychiatrist just didn't show up that week. Instead I was taken to see the prison doctor. He had no interest in my pleas for meds. "I don't want to listen to you anymore," he said, waving his hand like he was swatting away a mosquito. "Take him away." Then he hesitated, "But give him a shot of Valium first."

I'd never taken Valium before, and the speed with which it worked surprised me. Within a minute I was slumped on my chair, only able to get back to the cell by being held up and half dragged along by two guards.

It felt great. My panic was capped off, as if it belonged to someone else. I took up my usual routine in the courtyard, stumbling like a zombie for the next couple of hours.

As much as I liked the feeling of Valium working in my body, when it wore off I wanted more. The panic returned and the shaking resumed. When the guards next came to the door I knelt at the hatch and pleaded with them for help.

The next afternoon I was taken back to the clinic and given another shot of Valium. I spent the hours until the evening feeling numb and kind of relieved until gradually the drug wore off and panic started to eat its way through and grip me once again.

ON JUNE 5 Norine and I had our next open visit. It was her birthday, and we sat side by side on the bench. I'd brought a juice box and cookies with me so we could have Communion together. At the sight of Norine looking at me, the worry and pain etched deep on her face, I knew it was torture for her to see me like this, but I couldn't stop shaking.

"Norine," I said, my arms wrapped around my chest. I could feel between my ribs with my fingertips. "I don't trust myself anymore. I can't promise that I won't hurt myself. I need help. I'm trying to get medication."

After a week of daily shots, I finally got to see the prison psychiatrist. The drugs that I was prescribed—Xanax for my anxiety, antidepressants, plus something else to help me sleep—started working quickly. I felt calmer. I could still feel anxiety bubbling under the surface, but for the most part it didn't cross the Xanax barrier.

AT OUR NEXT VISIT, I could tell that Norine was relieved to see me looking better. I could even feel a smile forming on my face, and when I asked her how she was, she looked surprised.

For months I had used all my energy and focus to fight off the panic that was consuming me, but now with the meds restraining it I was able to look beyond myself more easily. The last few nights I had studied the picture we had taken together during the open visit on her birthday. She was the only woman in the world for me, the most beautiful one, but in that picture I could also see the tiredness, the pain, and knew she was in the fire with me. Now my heart was breaking for her too.

And for our kids. I cried as I thought of the time I was missing with them. I had not heard their voices in nine months. I knew it was hard on them too. Blaise especially was having difficulties, and I longed to be there for him. For the first time I heard that Jacqueline had married Kevin in a civil ceremony a few months before. Norine knew that I approved, but had kept this back from me because she thought it would make me sad. They would wait for me to have the wedding ceremony.

My wife had been reduced to praying, "Lord, if you don't do something, Andrew is going to take his life. I have prayed what I know to pray, others are praying, what can I do? *You* need to do something." Now, today, I had seen her cry for the first time in Sakran as she said, "I don't want to lose you." I couldn't bear to see her cry.

AS THE WORST OF THE PANIC SUBSIDED, so had the intensity of the suicidal urges. I was still on a daily roller coaster, but the highs and the lows were less jagged. Hundreds of times a day I breathed out, "God, I have no strength left. The only thing I can do is look to you for mercy. I can't hold on—you have to hold on to me." At the same time, I began to fight against the dark thoughts that had driven me to the edge. Every time I thought about suicide I declared the phrase Norine gave me—ordered me—to say: "Andrew in Christ chooses life."

What the Xanax could not do was deal with the grief deep inside of me. I very much wanted to live—but not like this. I would not kill myself, but I continued to ask God to do it for me: either send me home, or take me to heaven.

Several times I had heart palpitations. After the initial surge of adrenaline and fear, I would quickly switch to an expectant mode—maybe this was God answering my prayer.

The day the earthquake struck Sakran Prison most of the men ran out to the courtyard, but I stayed lying on my bunk and waited to see if the building would fall down on me. I just didn't care.

BUT EVEN AS I ASKED GOD for a mercy killing, I did not do it in anger or spite. I just couldn't imagine going on.

A tug-of-war intensified.

One Andrew started to pray, "Since I am suffering anyway, may it not be for nothing; complete the work you want to do in me." The other Andrew would say, "Who cares? Release me to my family or to heaven; I can't take this anymore."

These two Andrews were in a daily wrestling match with each other. And while one was wrestling with God, the other was trying to line up with God.

14 | A FURNACE OF FEARS

AS FAR AS I COULD TELL, I was the only man in the cell wrestling with my God. The others could not understand my anguish, my doubts, my cries to God. But I looked to him as a Father, and the silence and distance I was experiencing from him were deeply confusing. For my twenty-one cellmates, however, things were different. As Muslims they didn't share my expectation that God would comfort me with his presence, that he would demonstrate his love by letting me hear his voice even in prison. They were used to Allah's silence. They also believed this was their fate, decreed by Allah, and that following his rules in this time of testing would gain them favor on judgment day. And so they doubled down by throwing themselves into the rituals of their religion. These were serious Muslims, passionate about keeping the laws of Islam. Most of them had been so on the outside, and those who had not been became so in prison.

When I first arrived in the eight-man cell it was crowded, but at least it was possible for my eleven Muslim cellmates to lay out their mats upstairs in the sleeping area and pray together at the same time. Each of them was desperate to get out of prison and believed that the best way to persuade Allah to intervene on their behalf was to do all their prayers. When the others came and the cell was pushed beyond capacity, the only option was for the men to take turns. And so what started out as a thirty-minute prayer session five times a day became a rolling, intense nonstop prayer service.

It wasn't enough just to offer the standard prayers five times each day, or even to offer extra prayers. Soon they were extending their prayer times with periods of singing, reciting the names of Allah. Almost as soon as one group finished, another would start. Several times a day groups would form to chant the Koran. They'd sit in a circle, seven or eight men at a time, and take turns leading, reciting in Arabic. Relatively few Turks can read the Koran in Arabic, but everyone in our cell could—and those who had not known how were busy learning. At some point one of the men suggested that they should read through the entire Koran out loud each week, and the task was duly divided up among the cell. And when there wasn't a prayer or a chanting session taking place, the chances are that someone would be teaching others about the Koran.

Added to this, many of the men had their own personal routines. Someone read that reciting a particular chapter in the Koran fourteen times a day for a month, or repeating some prayer tens of thousands of times, would lead to release from prison—and so they set out to do this, on their bunks, in the courtyard, everywhere and all the time. Even in the middle of the night, there were usually some men who were fasting—and therefore sleeping during the daylight fasting hours—who would sit downstairs studying the Koran. There was hardly an hour, day or night, when there wasn't some religious activity happening in the cell.

I tried to ignore it, but inside or outside there was no escape from the sound of people praying and reading in Arabic or discussing in Turkish the steps required to unlock Allah's favor and secure their release.

I listened in silence one night early on as the conversation turned to Jesus. A couple of the men—who had already told me that I was the first Christian they had ever met—were talking at length about the failings of Christianity.

"The Bible has been changed," one said. "Jesus did not die on a cross. There are contradictions on every page. Christians will never admit this, but the whole book has been changed over the years."

"The Christians believe that Jesus, God, and Mary are all gods. And they deny that Abraham, David, and Jesus were all Muslims."

136

"Okay!" I mumbled to myself as I got up from my bunk and went downstairs. "Do you want to know what a Christian believes? Will you let me tell you?"

They sat in silence, staring.

So I carried on. I tried to explain the Jesus of the Bible in a way they would understand. I laid out the differences, being careful not to say anything about Muhammad that would offend any of them.

They listened. Some were genuinely curious, a couple of them looked on silently, unhappy, almost glowering. After a couple of hours I could tell I had said enough.

It was a turning point in the cell. Now they knew exactly where I stood, that I was serious about my faith. Some of them tried to encourage me to accept Islam—they certainly joked about it a lot. From that point on, whenever someone came and asked questions, two or three of the others would drift over and start to argue with me, bringing the conversation around to a lengthy discourse on the glories of Islam.

Eventually I got tired of this. When I was asked to explain some point yet again, I would pick up my Turkish copy of the Bible. "Please, read this first," I would say, pointing to a passage. "Then let's talk." If there was genuine curiosity or interest, I would be glad to answer.

Apart from Yilmaz, an older man on the bunk next to mine who read the whole Bible from cover to cover, most of them wouldn't even touch the book.

But most of them would accept prayer. When someone was sick I would put my hand on him and pray for healing. One of the men who was unfriendly had an old problem with his leg, and he let me pray for him several times. In return sometimes I would hear my name mentioned in the daily prayer for deliverance.

THE RHYTHM OF THE PRAYER CYCLES and the constant droning of Arabic chanting wore me down. It was like living in a mosque—but with more religious activity than a mosque, and much more intense. *La ilaha illalah, la ilaha illalah* . . . I had heard the phrase "There is no God

137

but Allah" chanted and sung so many times that it played on a continual loop in my mind night and day. Sometimes I thought it might be better to be in a solitary cell, just to get relief from this atmosphere that felt so heavy to me. I could still appreciate the way in which they were able to support each other, and I longed for the company of a fellow Christian in the cell—someone to pray with, someone to encourage me, someone to speak truth to me when my doubts started to scream. Norine was my lifeline, but I saw her for only the weekly thirty-five minutes. The rest of the time I was alone, so alone in my faith.

I'd lost Emin too. The other men in the cell were all public servants or small shop owners, and few of them had traveled outside of Turkey. Coming from a very wealthy family, Emin had spent time in the West and visited the US a number of times. Of everyone there he understood best the differences between my background and the others', and in those early days in Sakran he was the one who helped me to see how the cell operated and helped the cell to better understand me.

Emin had been released in February. I was glad for him, but sad to see him go. When he left I felt even more alone. Worse, though, was the fact that I no longer had someone who could help explain my "strange" American behavior and thinking to my Turkish cellmates. Emin's wealth and social position meant that the others listened to him. With him gone, I had lost my protector.

AS WELL AS PUTTING IN THE HOURS PRAYING, chanting, and studying the Koran, my cellmates were striving for ceremonial cleanliness. They had strict and detailed rules to follow so that their prayers would be acceptable. Along with washing in the correct manner before prayers, they also tried to avoid anything that would contaminate them and make them spiritually unclean. Most of the men in the cell were happy to leave me alone and ignore me, but for some, as a non-Muslim, I was a threat.

It started with food. Some mornings at roll call I would tear off a piece of bread from the end of the loaf to eat with some cheese before returning upstairs to bed. Sometimes I would throw away the last little bit of crust that I hadn't finished. One morning, one of the men who always had his eye on me decided to take offense.

"What you are doing is a sin, Andrew."

I ignored his comment and continued on back to bed. I knew he was picking on me. Every day the prison gave fresh bread, and at the end of each day the people in this cell quietly threw out all the leftover bread.

He said the same thing the next day. Again I ignored it and went back to bed.

The third time he caught me throwing a small piece of crust in the trash he turned to all the other men who had gathered for morning count by the guards.

"I would never throw that little bit of bread away," he said to nods of approval from the others. "It is a sin and you must stop."

"It might be a sin for you," I said, "but it isn't for me. Leave me alone." I needed to draw a line.

He backed off a little, but within weeks a new issue surfaced. We ate our salads and some other things from big communal bowls, each man dipping his spoon in and eating straight out of it in the normal Turkish way. I noticed that people would avoid taking food from the corner I'd put my spoon in. Eventually the inevitable happened and I was told that I was no longer welcome to eat from their bowls and that they would serve me separately.

"Fine," I said.

I was quite happy to eat off my own plate, but I did not like the reason for being excluded. There was a real mixture of attitudes in our cell. Most of the prisoners left me in my own bubble, and a few were helpful and even caring. One ex-policeman always offered me a hot cinnamon drink when he had his nightly tea, and a gentle schoolteacher who was an expert on the Koran cut my hair with the clipper our cell was allowed to buy. Kaya, a former police chief, often stopped by my bunk to give me an encouraging word. But there were some who treated me with suspicion, and their attitude began to infect others. They saw me as unclean and made me feel it.

Many of the men spent the evening and late into the night downstairs watching TV. Some of their favorite shows—each lasting up to four hours—were historical dramas that portrayed Christians as the evil aggressors always committing terrible acts against noble Turkish Muslims. The Christians in the stories were liars, treacherous, full of betrayal. During our years in Turkey we had good relationships with most Turks—we loved them, and on an individual level they were warm and welcoming to us—but I was very aware of an underlying animus toward Christians. Apart from this, for many years polls in Turkey had shown deep anti-American feeling, and it was growing.

Increasingly I felt singled out and isolated.

When someone said hard words to me I usually would apologize and remain silent. I tried to keep to myself and avoid things I knew would bother them. I was walking on eggshells. By late spring I wrote to Norine, "I speak maybe ten sentences a day. I'm trying to be invisible."

HOWEVER INTENSE THINGS WERE during those first months in Sakran, the atmosphere became more charged when Ramadan started at the end of May. My companions poured themselves out in prayer late into the night. The only positive was the fact that since they were all asleep during daylight hours I got to walk the courtyard mostly uninterrupted.

As the month of prayer and fasting wore on, the temperatures started to rise. On most days it was over one hundred degrees, and on the day it pushed as high as one hundred and sixteen it was hot as an oven. The only windows looked out onto the courtyard, all concrete and walls, and we were in the middle of multiple rows of sunbaked cells just like ours. In the airless cell, crammed for some time now with more than twenty sweaty bodies, the heat became oppressive. I found that the only way I could cope was to strip down to my shorts and lie on top of my covers.

This did not go down well with some.

My bunk was at the top of the stairs, so anyone who walked up or down had to pass right beside me. One day, not long before the end of Ramadan, one of the men told me that I needed to cover myself up.

"When we walk by you on the way to do our prayers we see you. You're distracting us and it's making us lose our ceremonial cleanliness."

I wanted to laugh out loud. "Why should you be distracted by me?"

"A man should cover himself from above the belly-button to the knees, Andrew. You need to wear long pants and a top."

Even stripped down I was soaking my bed and pillow with sweat and had a heat rash on my arms. I answered respectfully, but held my ground.

"I suggest you not look at me when you go by. It is very hot, so I do not want to wear long pants. Also, I am not a Muslim, so I am not required to follow your rules for dress."

The conversation died soon after, but the tension remained.

A COUPLE OF DAYS LATER, when several of the men had received bad news about their cases, they were talking animatedly in the courtyard. I was pacing as usual when one of them shouted at me. "You're done for the day. No more walking for you. Stop!"

I didn't stop. "I'm not in your way. Why are you giving me orders? What's going on?"

"I'll give you orders," he spat. "You're a *hayvan*!"

I stopped dead.

To call someone a *hayvan*—an animal—is a serious insult in Turkey. People kill each other over less. The guy wouldn't stop either, repeating the word over and over, telling me that I was filthy and unclean.

I was convinced that he was going to attack me. Through blurry eyes I watched him, his arms waving as he shouted, his eyes bulging. I looked at the others, wondering whether they would either join in or hold him back, but everyone was silent.

I was so fragile I retreated back to my bunk—the only safe place I had. The sense of isolation welled up and I started weeping, feeling the heavy sobs erupt from my chest. I tried to close my eyes and ignore the feelings of loneliness and despair, but it was no use. I was weak and defenseless, not just physically, but emotionally too.

That night the cell had a meeting about me.

The men who had called me an animal apologized—only after being told to by the others—and then launched into a speech about my character flaws. "You're a very selfish person, Andrew. You think you can make demands and have things your own way. Not anymore. It's over. You're going to do what we tell you."

I heard every word he said, but I wasn't thinking about change or the need for me to become more docile and accommodating to the group. All I could think about was that at some point, if things got much worse, the verbal attacks might stop. If some of the people in the cell decided to get physical with me, I'd be completely at their mercy.

15 | THE VALLEY
OF DRY BONES

THE RISING TENSION IN THE CELL underscored a worry that had begun to weigh on my mind.

When the foreign minister appeared on TV in May and accused me of supporting both FETO and the PKK, he painted a bull's-eye on me. It was one thing to hear my accusers make up stories about me being a Gulenist. My cellmates all knew very well that this could not be true, especially since some of them were linked to Gulen. Besides, they are an Islamist movement, meaning my work was completely at odds with theirs. But in previous years our work with refugees had brought Norine and me into contact with a lot of Syrian Kurds. Turks are very open to conspiracy theories, and the media was full of stories about me supporting the PKK and being a spy. I would be surprised if some of my cellmates were not starting to have doubts about me.

As soon as we had started working with Syrian refugees in 2014 we knew that we were taking a risk. We understood that it could cause us problems, result in more scrutiny for our ministry, and potentially be misunderstood, especially since many of them happened to be Kurdish. But we also saw an unusual opportunity. Syria was a closed Muslim country. It had been mostly inaccessible, but now several million Syrians had flooded into Turkey, fleeing the fighting in their country. We did not want to pass up this opening to reach them with our faith. The worst that we believed the government would do would be to deport us.

In 2014 we'd traveled to Gaziantep, a Turkish city close to the Syrian border, to lead a conference for around twenty Christians making the journey from Syria and Iraq. Some had been held at the border and beaten, only to make it through eventually by crawling through drainage pipes. Others had even walked through a minefield to get there. Their spiritual hunger really stirred me, but I was even more impressed that after the week of sessions they went back across the border to very difficult and dangerous places so they could minister to others. If they were willing to take such risks just to get training, then I should be willing to invest in them, even if it meant risk for us.

When the refugee crisis hit a few months later we started to work both in Izmir and on the Syrian border. Over the next two years I returned to the border area often, several times with Norine, and it always moved my heart to meet people who had lost so much in such terrifying circumstances. With a team that could speak Kurdish and Arabic we gave food and support, talked openly about our faith, had Bible studies with those who were interested, and when eventually some of the new Christians decided to return to Syria, we did what we could to send them back equipped. In Izmir our team started a refugee church and a number of people became Christians and were baptized. Right before our arrest we had joined around seventy refugees for a church retreat.

I have never sympathized with the PKK. Our goal is what it has always been—to tell people about Jesus, that's all. But the government was now lumping all the Kurdish refugees with the PKK, and I knew there were photos of me with Kurdish refugees. Given the political climate in Turkey, and considering all the lies being spread about me, I knew that our ministry could be used to harm me. And I could not be sure that everyone in the cell would think me innocent. Maybe I was being paranoid, but I no longer felt completely confident that I was safe in the cell.

WHEN I COULD, I read books by others who had been imprisoned to see if there was some secret I could learn. Kenneth Bae in North Korea seemed to have peace. Brother Yun in China said he experienced joy every day. Even though Dan Baumann in Iran had attempted suicide, he was later enthralled by a vision of the beauty of Jesus. There were Russians who had patiently endured the miserable prisons in Siberia.

This was *not* my experience.

"God picked the wrong man," I told Norine more than once.

"No," she'd say. "I think maybe he picked the right man. This was not an accident."

I knew that I did not measure up. But then I began to discover that some of the great Christians I admire had struggled. Adoniram Judson had thought about jumping off a bridge when he was being transported between prisons in Burma. Haralan Popov in Bulgaria and Helen Roseveare in Congo—in different places, but both with guns to their head—had begged for the trigger to be pulled.

I hadn't thought much about their despair before, but now I could relate in a new way to Elijah, Job, and Jeremiah, who had each wanted to die because of their troubles.

Although I would not put myself in the same league as any of these, I was relieved and strangely encouraged to know that I was not the only one to struggle.

EVEN SO, I WAS STRUGGLING to motivate myself to keep up my routines and disciplines. From early on at Sakran I had done some exercise at Norine's urging. I had filled a couple of small water bottles and used them as handheld weights to help strengthen my neck muscles after surgery. I did push-ups against the wall and walked for at least four hours a day. The walking was not to stay in shape—I needed to fill time, to wear myself out for sleep, to keep panic down. This was when I'd talk to God constantly. I worked out that at my average speed of three miles an hour I'd clocked up enough miles to get me from our home in North Carolina just about all the way to LA.

But when the mouth of hell opened up and the deal fell through, it all ground to a halt. I quit my calisthenics. I read my Bible less. I prayed less. I stopped writing letters to Norine every day. I stopped writing in my journal.

Walking was the last thing to go.

WHEN RAMADAN ENDED and my cellmates stopped sleeping most of the day, our relationship took yet another dive down.

I was no longer the only one who wanted to use the courtyard. My cellmates wanted to sit out in the shade and talk for hours on end, and they made it clear that they didn't want me pacing up and down. "Andrew, you can't go outside any more."

"What? Can't I just walk in the sun while you sit in the shade?"

"No. You're done here. We don't want to see you walking any more."

The meds stopped the panic from overflowing, but I could still feel it rise and surge inside me. If I was no longer allowed access to the courtyard I would effectively be confined to my bunk. I'd be trapped in a prison no bigger than my mattress.

I tried to persuade the men to reconsider but they refused. I asked to see the prison psychologist and pleaded my case with her, hoping that I might be able to use a different courtyard on my own for just a couple of hours a day. The best she could suggest was that I move to a solitary cell. "And if you're in solitary you only have access to a courtyard for one hour a day."

I had no choice but to stay. My world had been reduced to me, my bunk, and my fan. And even this was not secure. One of the men started talking in front of the others—"Andrew, we're going to take your fan away." I just stayed quiet. I'd soak my T-shirt under the tap, lie for an hour while the breeze cooled me down, then get up and wet my shirt again. Hour after hour I lay there and read.

I had just read that many people go into times of testing but do not make it out. I could imagine the valley of testing, littered with dry bones, the skeletons of those who had failed. I was so close to ending up there. I prayed, *Please, God, help me finish well.*

"Andrew!" I tried to ignore the voices calling my name. I focused on the fan—the sound of the blades in the air, the feel of the breeze on my skin. My T-shirt was almost dry. I'd have to wet it again soon.

"Andrew! Get down here."

It was a guard shouting this time, not one of my cellmates. Slowly I hauled myself up from my bunk and carefully walked downstairs.

One of the head guards was at the door. "Your transfer has come through."

I looked confused. I hadn't spoken with anyone about a transfer. I didn't want a transfer. Transfers were always bad news.

"I don't understand," I said. "What do you mean?"

"We're moving you. You're going to Buca."

PART FIVE

16 | MAXIMUM SECURITY

I STOOD IN THE ASSISTANT PRISON DIRECTOR'S OFFICE and breathed slow and deep as I begged to be allowed to remain at Sakran. I remembered all the stories my cellmates told about Buca when I first arrived, and I was desperate to avoid it. I knew that I was in no condition to move to an aging prison full of PKK fighters where for half the year the water was too cold to wash with and the days were spent huddling beneath whatever blankets you could find.

When I was done talking the prison director spread his hands and shrugged. "It has already been decided. You have to go."

The fear unraveled inside me again. "But what if it's overcrowded there? What if I'm put in a packed cell like the one here and there's no bed for me? If I have to sleep on a mattress on the floor they'll make me roll it up during the day, and then how will I spend my time if I can't walk outside? Or my meds? What if they won't let me have my meds there?" The words came tumbling out of me. I was fragile enough that any major change in routine sent me over the edge into panic.

"There's no discussion, Andrew. You're moving."

Back in the cell I started to gather my possessions. As soon as it became clear that I was leaving, the men who were sleeping on the floor started talking among themselves about who should have my bunk. A couple of the original guys who had treated me well said they were sad to see me go. They helped me throw my things in trash bags while the guards waited in the doorway. As I headed for the door I quickly hugged each of my twenty cellmates—including the ones who had criticized me and treated me as unclean.

Kaya, a kind man who had seen the warning signs of suicide in my early days and made sure I was not left on my own, put his hand on my shoulder when I was done. "Andrew, if they gave me a chance to go to Buca I would leave here in a heartbeat. It's much better."

I knew he was doing his best to encourage me and I appreciated it, but there wasn't a single cell in my body that believed him.

AT SOME POINT between leaving Sakran and driving up through the hills to the east of Izmir that lead to Buca Prison, I had a revelation. And while it didn't remove my fear of what lay ahead, it changed something in me.

Throughout the drive I tried to ignore the submachine guns slung over the laps of the military police guarding me. Instead I stared out the scratched-up window that formed one side of the prisoner bubble I was riding in. It was afternoon when we left Sakran and by the time we reached Izmir the streets were crowded with people beginning their journeys home.

Home.

The thought stabbed me at first. I was so far from home, so powerless to get there. My wife, my children had never felt so distant. But then a small ray of light broke through my sadness.

I looked at a man sliding past in a white VW Golf. He was totally oblivious to my presence. Like everyone else on the road, he was driving home to his family.

Ahead of him lay years of freedom. Ahead of me lay Buca. I didn't know if I'd ever be free again to be with my family. But while I knew nothing about his story, I knew something about mine: I knew Jesus. I may be a prisoner now, but I had the promise of eternal life, the guarantee of ultimate freedom.

My life had meaning.

My life was not empty.

My suffering was not the end of my story.

WHEN WE ARRIVED AT BUCA I could tell we were in the mountains. It was hot, but not as hot as Sakran. If nothing else, I was grateful for that. I could also tell that the men in my old cell were right. Sakran was a sprawling, modern, high-tech prison. Buca was older and more austere.

The arrival routine was much the same as it had been at Sakran. I was handed over to the guards, taken to a side room, and searched. The assistant prison director was a large, gray-haired man. There was no question he was in charge, but he seemed more relaxed than the directors I'd met at Sakran. He ran his hands over my possessions that were laid out on the table before me—the books and clothes that I'd been allowed in the cell, plus the various items that the authorities had kept back from me, like my wallet, IDs, and passport. It was strange seeing those forbidden items. With each move they felt less and less like mine.

When I was in Sakran Norine had fought hard for me to be allowed to have a Bible and other books in English. It had taken months but eventually someone had managed to get approval from Ankara. I wondered how long it would take in Buca before I'd be allowed to have them again.

"Please," I said. "If I'm going to be placed in solitary at first, could I take my Bible and another book? It's hard to be on my own without anything to read."

The prison director stepped back from the table and weighed my request, letting the silence hang in the air. Finally, he said, "Okay."

I gladly picked up my Bible as well as the biggest book I could find, a fist-thick novel by Tom Clancy.

The director dismissed me and I walked in silence behind the guards to my cell. It was a similar setup to Sakran—the self-contained cells all had their own courtyards—but there was one major difference. Buca was a maximum-security prison. The logic was that in a prison full of people accused of terror offenses and the worst crimes committed, the greatest risk wasn't so much in them escaping but in violence, or the inmates spreading their ideology among others. The more dangerous or valuable the prisoner, the fewer other prisoners he should be with. In Buca the cells were made for three people, and they were keeping the cells at three, unlike Sakran where twenty or more inmates were crammed into each cell.

"You'll stay here for a while," said the guard as he showed me into the cell. I noticed that unlike Sakran, where the guards always seemed tense and hard, the two who showed me into my cell in Buca appeared just a little more relaxed.

When the door shut and locked behind the guards, I felt the silence weigh heavy upon me. Sakran was busy and loud, not only inside the cell but also out in the corridors as the guards came and went all through the day and night. Buca was different. There was nothing to hear apart from the distant whir of a generator.

Within an hour my door was thrown open. "We're moving you," said a different guard, almost smiling. "We phoned Sakran and they told us about you. They said not to leave you alone. Grab your things now, we're putting you in with someone else."

I grew more nervous with every step. Even though I knew it was better to be with someone than in solitary, my mind taunted me about who I was about to be placed with. Would he be a hardliner who would take offense at my faith? An aggressive nationalist who would be angry at an American, especially one accused of being a spy?

The guard unlocked my new cell and I stepped in.

The man inside looked harmless, like the kind of Turkish neighbor who would be quick to drop everything he was doing and sit and drink tea with his guest. He greeted me with a half smile as he studied my face.

"I know you," he said once the guards had left. "I've seen your story on TV."

I waited for his verdict.

"Welcome! I'm Ramazan. Do you prefer I call you Rambo Priest or just plain Andrew?"

OVER THE NEXT FEW DAYS I found out more about Ramazan. He was a lawyer who handled some work for Asya Bank, which was linked to Fethullah Gulen. He also had ByLock on his phone, so according to the authorities there was more than enough reason to consider him a high-security prisoner and hold him for more than a year without trial. But while my cellmates in Sakran had often been angry about their cases and were desperate to get things moving, Ramazan in many ways had accepted that he was powerless to change his situation and knew that all he could do was wait.

I LIKED RAMAZAN, but I was still on edge.

The move left me shaken psychologically, upsetting my already fragile spiritual state. I felt like I had no anchor, as if God wanted me to be in a position where everything was completely dark and unknown. I could see that my cell situation was better in Buca, but I was fearful that being in a maximum-security prison would eventually mean trouble for me. Either they'd be stricter with me—like giving me less access to Norine—or the move was an ominous sign that the government was going to double down and dream up some new, more serious charges against me.

As part of my intake I was taken to the prison psychologist. I told her I was very stressed about my wife not knowing I had been moved. She picked up a pen. "Give me her number and I'll call her later. I'll let her know you're here." A couple of hours later I was surprised when a guard came to our cell to tell me Norine had been contacted. Knowing that eventually I would see her eased my mind. In Sakran no one ever, ever told us anything.

But then I was taken to the prison psychiatrist.

I told him about my medication in Sakran and how much it helped.

It was going okay, until our session came to a close. "These meds they put you on," he said, confidently. "You don't need them. I am sure you can do without them."

I pushed back instantly. "No," I said. "I really can't. I've had frequent panic attacks and was suicidal before I started on them. Ever since starting the meds I've been much better. Stopping isn't an option for me."

He nodded at the guards to take me away. "I think you'll be fine. We'll start cutting your dose down."

Back in the cell I tried to push down the fear of losing my meds. I had learned that in prison, no matter how urgent a need may be, there was nothing I could do to tell anyone outside until I had a visit. I had to be patient and wait for someone to show up.

THE NEXT DAY, sooner than I had expected, I was taken out of the cell to meet with my lawyer. Suna was concerned when I told her about the psychiatrist and promised to tell Norine so she could follow up with the embassy. "I'm worried," I said, trying to hold my voice steady. "This is not the kind of place they let you out from. This is where they send you when they want to forget about you for years and years. This place is tougher than Sakran."

Suna shook her head. "No, Andrew. We think this is a positive move for you. They may have moved you for your own security."

"How is that good news for me?"

"They know that if anything happens to you there will be consequences. You're more valuable now. Maybe they moved you here to keep you safe."

I wasn't so sure myself.

But when Norine came to visit two days later, she brought the same message as Suna. She told me that the visiting policy was much better—that we'd be allowed a full hour together instead of the usual thirty-five minutes at Sakran.

"We think this is going to be better, my love," she said cautiously.

Maybe she was right. Buca was maximum security, but I was beginning to feel the difference between the intensity of the overcrowded cell in Sakran and living only with Ramazan. Now I could be alone, in quietness, most of the time. But there was another person around, which kept me from the fear that I felt in solitary.

I still had my doubts, though. "Why would God be setting me up in a better place? What if I've been sent here because God knows that I couldn't survive long term in a place like Sakran? What if he's setting me up for a long imprisonment?"

I wanted to allow her and Suna's optimism to encourage me. But I'd allowed myself to find hope behind bars before. It hadn't worked out so far.

17 | A NEW TRAJECTORY

I HAD ARRIVED AT BUCA A BROKEN MAN. But now I did something that changed my trajectory.

I realized I could not do much to fight for my freedom, but I could fight for my faith. If I did not survive spiritually, I knew I would lose everything. I had spent so many hours pacing the courtyard or lying on my bunk, accusing God, confused, and often angry and offended at him. But now I made a solemn decision, and announced it to God, almost in defiance: *Whatever you do or do not do, I will follow you.*

This became the basis of my declaration, and I added to it.

If you do not speak to me, I will follow you.

If you do not let me sense your presence, I will follow you.

If you do not show your gentleness or kindness, I will follow you.

If you allow me to be deceived, I will follow you.

If you leave me in prison, I will follow you!

I had no illusion that I could make it without God's help. But insofar as it was up to me, I determined to persevere.

I made a decision: *I will not give up!*

I may be terrified, I may be weak, I may be broken, but I am going to hold on.

I will look to Jesus, not away from him. I will run to Jesus or, if necessary, crawl to Jesus.

EVERY PRISON MAKES ITS OWN RULES, within certain parameters. One of the most important differences from Sakran was that Buca did not require me to write in Turkish. They had a guard who could read English, and he was tasked with checking all my mail, incoming and outgoing. This meant that others could now write to me, and as a bonus, Robert from the consulate was able to bring typed notes to me on his visits. The prison checked them, and the guard got them to me within a day or so. It was like a treasure each time. I would quickly scan the pages Norine had collated for me, then pace myself and read them slowly over two or three days, savoring them.

Most significant of all, I could write in English to my children. During my time in Sakran I had been so distraught that I had almost nothing to give to my family. But in Buca Norine laid out the truth: the kids needed to hear from me. So I started to engage. I needed to be a father to my beautiful children, even though I could not see them and was missing so much in their lives. I did not know when I would be with them, so I started to think of the legacy I wanted to leave them. My letters gave an opportunity to encourage and affirm them, to speak into their lives, to give them my blessing and love. I wrote about the things I wanted them to learn, how to interpret what was happening to me, how they should respond to suffering, and the hopes I had for their lives.

While I was at Sakran, Jacqueline had told Norine that if I wasn't released soon she would come to see us in the summer. We were concerned for her safety, because the Turkish government sometimes had imprisoned a man's innocent children or elderly parents, so we knew they were capable of using our children as leverage. But even though she was afraid, Jacqueline said, "I'm coming!" I thought the fact that her husband, Kevin, was in the US military would deter Turkey from arresting her. We felt better about Blaise coming, because we thought it unlikely they would do anything to a minor child in a case with this high a profile, but we told Jordan not to come. In the end we had bought tickets for Jacqueline and Blaise and got permission from Ankara for them to come to my next open visit.

Two weeks before my open visit at Sakran they moved me to Buca. We worried we would lose our visit because Buca scheduled theirs on the odd rather than even months, but the prison director agreed to allow it to go ahead. And so, two weeks after my transfer, the day of the visit finally arrived.

I had mixed feelings. Of course I longed to see my kids and hug them, but I didn't want them to see me in such a broken state.

The guards came to get me, but instead of taking me to the room used for visits they led me to the one they used for my meetings with Suna. It had a desk that cut the small room in half and foam padding on the walls to reduce the echo and make it easier for them to record the conversation.

I dug my heels in and refused to go inside. "The director told me I can have an open visit. I'm not going in that room!"

One of the guards waved a clipboard at me. "This is the room you're using."

"But I want to be able to hold them and hug them. I want to talk to the director."

The guard stared at me with cold contempt. "No. This is what you get," and pushed me in.

Norine was already there, vehemently arguing the same thing with the guard on her side of the room. It had been almost a year since I'd last seen Jacqueline and Blaise. I rushed toward them, and tried reaching over the desk to hug them, but it was awkward. Finally I decided to push the rules. I jumped up on the desk, swung my legs over to their side, and had them join me on the desk. I knew there were guards watching through the glass, and they might become angry, but I did it anyway. All that mattered was that for a while at least I got to sit beside my two kids, hugging them tight and feeling their sobs mixed with mine.

I felt like a father again.

I HARDLY GOT OUT OF BED for three whole days after the visit. I replayed every minute of it, how we'd said over and over that we loved each other. Blaise's final words—"I love you. Hang in there, Dad."—stayed with me so clearly. I could still hear them. Still feel them.

I was so glad to have seen Jacqueline and Blaise, but I felt so helpless too. I could feel the familiar despair leak into me again, and the old questions about God resumed.

Was God thwarted? If so, has he so limited himself that he cannot save me? And if he was not thwarted—what happened? Why did he allow me to be so deceived—if I was deceived? Why has he withheld any sense of his presence? Why did he let me be broken so completely?

These questions were suffocating my relationship with God. I did not choose to dwell on them—they were there, they wouldn't leave, they dominated, and I couldn't escape them. And they kept me from receiving truth and encouragement from God, from the Bible, from Norine, from any source.

I had read a book by Dan Baumann in which he explained how, after suffering a great disappointment with God, he locked away his questions in an imaginary box. I decided to do the same thing. I imagined a modern, high-tech safe with a hand scanner on the front as well as a turn handle. God and I were the only ones able to open it. I took each of my questions and doubts and deliberately placed them in the box.

"God," I prayed as I imagined myself sealing the lid shut. "I am locking these questions away. I am not going to ask them anymore, I am not going to demand answers. I do not understand, I am confused, and I am hurt. But these questions and doubts will remain in this box until a different time. You can open this box if you want, but I am leaving it sealed. I don't need to know the answers in order to continue my relationship with you."

From this point on whenever one of these questions came to mind, I would banish it back to the locked box.

EVEN THOUGH IT WAS COOLER up in the mountains than it was back in Sakran, I had no fan in Buca. My sheets were often soaked with my sweat, and I'd get heat rashes throughout the day on my neck, chest, stomach, and inner arms. At Sakran, even with meds the intensity of the crowded cell had kept me on edge and wrecked my sleep. But now the nervous energy had yielded to lethargy, and I dozed in and out for up to ten hours a day. Each day I'd look forward to the evening, when the air would begin to cool and I knew that soon I would be able to escape to some degree the stress that surrounded me by drifting off to sleep. This was my most peaceful time. It was also when I felt my strongest, and I could say, "Yes, Jesus, I am willing to suffer for you." But I knew that in the morning I'd wake up and feel the fear, the dread, and the monotony of life behind bars start to batter at my heart all over again.

I would have to start fighting again to refocus on God and keep this up deliberately throughout the day. I tried to make my time—from morning to night, whenever I was awake—as God-oriented as I could.

RAMAZAN AND I were reading on our bunks one morning when the slot in the door clanged open. "Get your things together, Andrew. We're moving you," said one of the guards. "There's a new directive that foreigners need to be in the same cell. So we're moving you in with a German."

"No! Please, no!" I said, scrambling to my feet. "I like Ramazan, I've just gotten used to him. I don't want to start over. And I don't speak German!"

When I'd finished protesting they agreed to ask the director, who sent them back to tell me that he was willing to compromise and move the German in with Ramazan and me. Before the end of the day the cell door opened and we were joined by Nejat—a bear of a man over six feet tall with a thunderous voice.

Nejat was Turkish born and raised but had studied engineering in Germany. He was a businessman who had taken up German citizenship, and like both of us he was accused of supporting Fethullah Gulen. But unlike so many of the others, Nejat admitted that he had participated in meetings, although he insisted—and rightly so—that he had done nothing illegal.

I liked Nejat. He had traveled and lived in a Western culture so I was not an object of curiosity. At the same time, he was very fervent in his faith. Almost as soon as Nejat arrived I noticed a change in Ramazan. He instantly became more animated, laying out his prayer mat before dawn and kneeling next to Nejat, praying louder than I'd heard him pray before. In my early morning haze I thought of some of the friends I would most like to have in prison with me. I so missed being with other Christians, and it gave me a new appreciation for the church.

At first I wondered if the cell might go the same way it did in Sakran, with me becoming even more of an outsider. And when Ramazan reminded me not to cross his field of vision anywhere in front of his mat while he was praying, I thought, *Oh, well . . .*

"That's wrong," bellowed Nejat. "The area on my prayer rug is the holy space, not the space in front."

Nejat didn't just stop at correcting and encouraging Ramazan. He frequently turned his attention to me, his deep voice rolling through the cell as he shared his opinion on my predicament.

"You need to stop stressing, Andrew. Stop thinking about the news, trying to figure out every new thing that happens. Stop worrying about the politics and what is going on. It doesn't matter what Trump says and it doesn't matter what Erdogan says. When God says you will come out you will come out. Until that day you aren't going anywhere, so don't even think about what anyone is doing!"

His words were just what I needed. "You know, Nejat," I told him a few times, "you'd make a better Christian than I do."

He'd brush away my words with his big hand. "We're both being tested, Andrew. And God is in charge. That's all there is to say."

WHEN NEJAT AND RAMAZAN weren't praying they'd often be in front of the TV. I wasn't the chess player Ramazan had hoped for, and between the stress and the sluggishness caused by my meds, which had been continued, I just didn't have enough interest to maintain the focus required to follow TV dramas in Turkish. Plus it was painful to watch normal life, knowing that it was going on without me. Sometimes they watched a house-hunting show taking place in North Carolina, not only close to home but the kind of show Norine and I used to enjoy together. What energy I had I put into the one thing I knew was essential for me: pressing into God.

Norine and I made a plan. As a family we would focus our prayers especially on one person each day, starting with the youngest—Blaise on Monday, then Jacqueline, Jordan, Kevin, and Norine on Friday. Since we were scattered in three countries, we picked a time we would all pray—8:00 p.m. Turkey time. We were trying to bring the family together. I started to fast two days a week—one day for the kids, and one day for Norine because she was carrying such a heavy load. I also agreed with her on a daily reading plan, and each evening I'd sit on my bed and open my Bible to Psalms. Even though we were separated I felt closer to her knowing that we were reading the same thing.

By now the Turkish government had canceled her yearlong visa and she was only allowed to apply for three-month visas. We held our breath each time she requested an extension. As our wedding anniversary approached, I was struck again with just how grateful I was for my wife. I wrote to her:

> *I was thinking today especially of our upcoming anniversary when I won the lottery and married you. Thank you for twenty-eight years—especially this last one that has been the most difficult. I think that I would not be alive now if you had not provided the encouragement, truth, the occasional correction/rebuke (never resented, you should know), and frequent reminders of your love for me. Thank you for your faithful love, for fighting for me, waiting for me, suffering with me.*

PLAYING THE GUITAR was another positive step that I took in Buca. On her first visit to the new prison, Norine was surprised to see "classical guitar" on the list of approved items—along with canaries!—so she immediately set out to find one. The first I knew of it was when the guard showed up at my cell the next day. "Here Andrew," he said, holding up a guitar. "Your wife brought this to you." Norine encouraged me to play it every evening. I had led worship with a guitar for years, but this seemed so distant now, and I did not feel like singing. But I carried on, as a discipline. I was determined to reclaim a part of me that existed long before I was a prisoner and to worship, even from a broken heart.

Most unusual of all, I had started dancing. I had been reading about Richard Wurmbrand, a Romanian pastor who was imprisoned and tortured for fourteen years under the communist regime. He took Jesus's words "rejoice and be exceedingly glad" as a direct command and chose to rejoice by dancing in his cell, in spite of the horrors he was facing.

I decided to do the same. I felt no joy and my body was weak and my spirit sad, but there was something about Wurmbrand's story that captivated me. It also convicted me, as I realized how far I was from Jesus's words that specifically said we should rejoice when persecuted. So I decided to dance like Wurmbrand danced. Each day, for a minimum of five minutes, I would leap around the courtyard. No matter how much I didn't feel like doing it, how hot the sun or how cold the rain, I danced. It was an act of the will.

Norine told me, "I am sure that when you get up to dance, the courtyard is full of angels who are following your lead." And I know Father God was pleased. As for Ramazan and Nejat, they just cast sidelong glances at me.

ON AUGUST 24, six weeks after I'd been moved to Buca, the guards came to my door and told me to get ready. Norine was due at the prison for our weekly visit, but that was at least an hour away. I looked at them, confused. "My wife's here already?"

"No. You've got a court appearance in ten minutes. Let's go."

I followed them to a small room where a video camera and TV screen were set up in a booth. I could see the judge and as soon as I sat down he started proceedings. I interrupted. "Sir, I'm not going to participate in anything without my lawyer."

The judge paused and stared at me. "We'll appoint you a lawyer then."

At the start of all this I would have given in. I would have agreed, hoping that by not putting up a fight I might earn their goodwill. But I was done with all that. "No," I said. "I want *my* lawyer."

The judge looked annoyed and ordered that I be taken back to my cell.

Within the hour I was being marched back to the video room. "Excuse me," I told the guard before he closed the door on me. "My wife is coming to visit me today and I don't want to miss that. Please can you have her wait if I'm not ready?"

This time I could see my lawyer, Suna, on the screen as well. She looked harried and the judge ran through proceedings faster than ever. The whole thing was strange and rushed.

"Andrew Brunson, there are new charges against you. Attempt to overthrow the government. Attempt to overthrow the constitutional order. Attempt to overthrow the parliament. In addition you are charged with military espionage. The original terrorism charges are still in place. What do you say?"

At first I had nothing to say. I had heard every word that the judge had said, but I was stunned. Could they really be talking about *me* and these crimes in the same breath?

Military espionage carried a twenty-year sentence, while each of the first three charges I was now facing carried an aggravated life sentence. That meant solitary confinement, with one hour's exercise each day, one phone call every two weeks, and an open visit every two months. For the rest of my life!

I felt indignation begin to boil in me. I leaned into the microphone and shot out my words. "When and how have I engaged in military espionage? Why would I support an Islamist movement? I want the government to explain this to me."

The judge said nothing.

"This is an insult to me and to my faith. I came to Turkey with one sole purpose, to explain Jesus Christ. And I did this openly."

"Anything else?"

"You make general accusations, but you don't ask about anything specific. When? Where? With whom? I have no way of knowing what I am supposed to give an answer for."

My protest didn't make any difference. It barely made them pause. Instead the judge waved me away. "You are now arrested under these charges."

THE GUARDS took me—frustrated and fuming—to see Norine. In God's mercy they'd kept her back to see me, but there was little to smile about. When I finished telling her what had happened we both sat in silence, eyes locked through the glass that separated us.

Fear had invaded every part of my body. It had saturated every breath I took.

"Do you realize what this means, Norine? I'd been thinking that maybe I was facing ten to fifteen years. But this is a whole other level. Even if they just convict me of one of these political crimes, it is life without the possibility of parole. They'll never let me go."

Norine held her hand up to mine against the glass. She told me that CeCe at the ACLJ had said that in cases like mine people are often found guilty before they're released, but her words sounded distant and too far away.

"What if the US government believes them? Do they know the courts are completely politicized? They won't fight for me any more if they think I'm caught up in all this."

She couldn't hold me—all she could do was press her hand tighter against the glass.

"It's not enough to humiliate and hurt me. They know I'm innocent, but they want to destroy me. How can I make it, Norine?"

18 | HEARTSONG

ON AUGUST 25, the day after I found out about the new charges against me, I didn't read any Scripture. I didn't touch the guitar or lift even one foot in dance. I was hit hard. I had been picking myself up over the last few weeks, but this news had slammed me down again, and there was such a heaviness hanging over me that I spent the entire day in bed. I could not get past the thought that I could spend the rest of my days in prison. Even as I'd been taken to the video booth there had been a part of me that wondered whether I was about to be released. This crash was brutal. I wondered when—if ever—God would say, "Enough!" And yet I knew that I had to get up again.

There was more news that came out the day after the court appearance. It was late in the afternoon and Ramazan was watching TV when I heard a report on a new government announcement. "Decree 694, Article 74, gives the President authority to exchange or return prisoners to their home countries if it is in the interest of Turkey."

Instantly I knew that this related to me, and I understood why the judge had been in such a rush to issue these new charges. By increasing my possible sentence from the original fifteen years to three life sentences plus a further twenty years, they were trying to raise the stakes. And if the US was in any doubt, the decree made it clear that it was perfectly possible for President Erdogan to grant my release, as long as he got something worthwhile in return. But there was no hurry for him—the same day they also decreed that prisoners could now be held without trial for seven years.

I once read that even one minute of horror—of intense fear—leaves the body exhausted. It is true. In the aftermath of the new charges I felt shattered. I struggled beneath the weight of what felt like a death sentence. By the third day, I forced myself to start to dance and pick up the guitar and worship, but in the long afternoons I'd be close to panic and despair. I would read my Bible, meditate, and pray, but at any point dread could pounce.

When I read that people were praying or that some were even looking at me as a role model I felt encouraged to press on. A dear friend had written to remind me to live for eternity. He mentioned the great cloud of witnesses that has gone on before me, but what caught my attention more was that a great number are also coming behind me. This impressed on me the need to be a good example, and so I would refocus, decide to persevere, and even though I felt alone, I would declare, "I am not alone." This was my daily roller coaster. I would get knocked down, but I was not staying down as long as I had in the past.

FROM THIS VERY DARK TIME came one of my most important victories.

It was in the afternoon one day early in September, a couple of weeks after my court appearance. I was walking round and round in the courtyard, overwhelmed by the idea of my years stretching out in lonely silence as I wasted away. I opened my mouth to pray, to pour out my feelings, but instead of accusation or complaint, something entirely different came out.

You are worthy, worthy of my all.

I started to sing these words, over and over. In my heartache I was declaring that Jesus was worthy of whatever I may suffer, and as I did more words came:

But my heart faints, drowned in sorrow, overwhelmed
Make me like you, Cross-bearer, persevering, faithful to the end.

I bared my heart to Jesus. I knew that I'd come so close to giving up on so many different occasions. I desperately needed him to transform me so that I could end my race like he did.

When I stopped singing, the song carried on, growing within me with new verses. For a couple of days I carried it around with me before eventually writing it down and adding some chords on the guitar. This was my heartsong, a love song to God from the deepest part of me.

I'd passed so much of my time in Sakran in a fog of panic, but in Buca I was able to think back with a little more clarity on my journey so far. I remembered a very low point when I said to God, "Whatever things you have planned for me, however you want to use me, I give it up. I don't care if I have no reward in heaven. Just take me back to my family. I can't handle this anymore." But these lyrics showed how much had changed in me:

I want to be found worthy to stand before you on that day
With no regrets from cowardice, things left undone
To hear you say, "Well done, my faithful friend, now enter your
    reward"
Jesus, my Joy, you are the prize I'm running for

I did not want to get to heaven and have regrets about the choices I'd made on earth. I could picture standing before Jesus and him showing me things that he had wanted to accomplish through me, but that I missed out on. I had no doubt I could still be a coward. But I was determined that my emotions would not have the final word. I was declaring with my will that I wanted to embrace whatever assignments God had for me—even prison, if necessary.

From then on, I sang my song to God every day.

As the year anniversary of my arrest approached, the diplomatic efforts seemed to be going in circles. Norine had heard that President Trump had spoken with Erdogan, arguing for my release. When Erdogan had repeated the charges against me about being a terrorist and spy, Trump's response was vehement and forceful: "Cut the BS. We know it's not true."

Within weeks of my new charges and the announcement of Decree 694, Erdogan was publicly offering to swap me for Fethullah Gulen. They had been asking the US to extradite him. "Give Gulen to us," he said in a televised speech to police officers at the end of September. "Then we will try Brunson and give him to you."

Finally what I had known for a long time was out in the open. While the Turkish government had been insisting publicly that I was just another terrorist going through a normal judicial process, behind the scenes they had been making demands from a long and impossible "ask list." We heard that at one point President Trump had said, "Ask me for something I *can* give you." The Turks had come close to an agreement many times but kept changing their minds. Now the truth became plain for everyone to see: I was being held only at the whim of President Erdogan.

Hearing my case raised by Erdogan like this did not make me feel confident. It was clear that I was a political hostage, and I lost count of the number of times that Ramazan or Nejat would call up from downstairs and tell me that some journalist or other was talking about me again. At first I'd go watch or listen in, but soon I gave up taking much notice of it altogether.

The stress of the case had started to show on Suna. She had worked hard for us all along, but her name was starting to show up in the media. The reality of Turkey in 2017 was that lawyers were being thrown in prison if they defended the wrong person. We understood completely when she stepped away from my case in September.

When Norine started the search for a new lawyer, she discovered just how politically untouchable I had become. A few offered to take me on but only if we paid astronomical fees. Thankfully, after a few weeks we found a new lawyer. Cem was an Armenian Christian based in Istanbul, and he was recommended as the kind of bold, strong lawyer who would fight for us.

Besides the pressure of finding a new lawyer, I was concerned that my own government might tire of working on my case and move on to something else. Back in July, CeCe had told us there was unprecedented interest and effort by Congress and the administration to free me. I was aware that President Trump was continuing to raise my case in conversations with Erdogan, and my release was part of a wider discussion with Turkey about a number of issues, including Syria. But weeks went by and there was very little sign of progress. The Turks were immovable. How long would my government keep up their efforts? And there were always whispers in my mind that they might start to believe the accusations about me and quietly back off.

On October 5, when two members of USCIRF (the United States Commission on International Religious Freedom) visited me along with a US consular official, I got some much needed reassurance. Kristina Arriaga and Sandra Jolley were two firebrands who seemed genuinely shocked when I asked the consul if they believed I was innocent. Kristina looked me in the eye. "Of course you're not guilty," she said emphatically while tears wet my face.

ONE MORNING, Ramazan announced that he had submitted a request to have our photograph taken, and the guards would be here soon. When they showed up we followed them out to the courtyard and lined up together for a picture of the three of us. I then asked the guard to take an individual shot of me.

I stood against the courtyard wall.

The guard eyed me suspiciously. "What's that you're holding?"

It was a small cross that a Chinese Christian had given to me before my arrest. I was holding it so that it fell over my hand, which was covering my heart.

"You can't take a picture with a cross. No religious symbols allowed."

"Please," I said. "Take the picture. Your supervisor can delete it if he wants, but please take it."

I have no idea why he gave in, but he did. And in that bleak courtyard I felt something that I had not experienced in the whole year that I had been held hostage. Happiness. I wasn't carefree and I wasn't about to burst out in laughter. But somewhere inside me, quiet but strong, I was happy. I was declaring who I was, proudly holding a cross that reminded me of all my fellow Christians who had been persecuted for their faith. I embraced my identity.

I belonged to Jesus Christ.

I was Andrew of the cross.

If you look, you can see it in my eyes.

I HAD REALLY WANTED THAT PICTURE for Norine and our kids. I wanted this to be how they saw me. And on our next visit, the guard passed it on to Norine.

Those visits were so important for me. The encouragement I received in that one hour had to last me for the next 167 hours. Toward the end of our visit I would always ask the same question: "Do you believe I will come out?"

"I do," she'd say. "I just don't know when."

This was always followed by: "Why do you think I'll come out?" I knew what her answer would be, but needed to hear it anyway.

"For two reasons. Andrew, think of all the words about our future that God gave us before this started. They can't all be wrong. I believe you have a future outside of prison. And second, God has raised up a huge movement of prayer, and he is going to answer it. He just hasn't done it *yet*. People are *still* praying. In places like Vanuatu in the South Pacific, Indonesia, Senegal, Bolivia . . . It's absolutely supernatural. God is waking some up in the middle of the night to pray for you . . . Just hold on!"

And finally, I could not resist asking: "Do you think it will be a long time?"

I had felt so alone through my imprisonment, and I still did. But more and more I was aware that there were many believers around the world joining me in my cell each day. I had several dozen pictures from Brazil of groups praying for me in churches and home groups and in children's Sunday school classes. I was so grateful for the family of God.

I TRIED NOT TO BE TOO MOVED by the ups and downs of political developments, but they did affect me emotionally because I knew that any new difficulty between the two countries made my situation harder.

When Erdogan had been in Washington for the summit, some members of his security team had assaulted protesters on the street outside the Turkish embassy in DC. Arrests had followed and the whole thing threatened to become yet another thorn in the relationship.

Reza Zarrab and Hakan Atilla, Turkish citizens, were also due to go on trial in the US soon in a case of helping Iran evade sanctions. Almost certainly this would cause serious embarrassment to the Turkish government.

In October, the US government announced that it was ceasing to issue visas to Turkish citizens after Turkey arrested a second US consulate local employee. This move actually presented an unusual opportunity for my situation also to be resolved before visas resumed. It was the first time the US was moving beyond diplomatic talk regarding the unlawful arrests. We watched and waited. But visas were resumed before the new year. Nothing had changed.

AND SO TIME PASSED.

As Christmas drew near I told Norine: "If I'm still here at Christmas I'll thank Jesus for coming to this earth. If I'm still here at New Year's, I will thank him for bringing me through this year. If I'm still here on my birthday, I will thank him for the life that he gave me."

Our daughter graduated from university and Norine could only cry, watching the livestream.

I spent another Christmas in prison. Norine sent me a nice, soft scarf, something to keep me warm in the cold, but also something visible that would remind me of her love. She told me, "Feel my arms around your neck each time you wear it."

In January I turned fifty.

Norine's father died, but she didn't go to the funeral because she was afraid she would not be allowed back in to Turkey.

And every day brought the same struggle until I reached a place where I was willing to embrace God's assignment for me.

IN EARLY FEBRUARY 2018, Norine told me she would be going to Ankara to meet with Wess Mitchell, assistant secretary of state. The relationship between Turkey and the US had been going from bad to worse over my whole imprisonment. An official told us, "If someone wanted to write a movie script about the relations they couldn't make it any worse." Norine especially kept her eye on the relationship because even though not one of these issues had anything to do with us, they all affected our situation. Tillerson was returning to Ankara to meet with Erdogan and to work to put things right. They met for three and a half hours.

When Norine visited next the news was encouraging. "I was told that the meeting went well, that this is good for the relations between the countries and could lead to good developments for you. They think your situation could be resolved soon. And the day after the meeting they released a German journalist who had been held for a year. He was indicted and released pending trial, and they let him leave the country the same day. Maybe this is how they'll do it with you, my love."

A State Department official suggested to Norine that she ask contacts in Congress to hold off on sanctions they were going to introduce against Turkey. Things looked positive right now, and sanctions could backfire. Norine followed this recommendation.

We were both cautiously optimistic, but in the run-up to Tillerson's visit, Karakaya had come to the prison to interrogate me. I'd asked him to drop the charges—after all, we both knew I was innocent. But he puffed his cheeks and waved my request away. "Certainly not," he said. "We have over forty binders of information on you." Forty binders? He had to be bluffing, but even so it bothered me. And the timing was significant. What had set Karakaya in motion? It was political signaling by the Turkish government ahead of Tillerson's visit. It could be good . . . or bad.

THE HOPE THAT I'D BEEN FEELING took a blow a few weeks later when Tillerson was let go. It would take time for his replacement to be confirmed, and the road map that had already been agreed on might possibly change. I felt like I had been returned to the same place as when I was first arrested and everything was on hold before the inauguration.

But Tillerson's departure wasn't the only thing to worry about. Amid the hope that somehow, finally, this was all going to come to an end, Norine heard something that made her angry but not surprised. Someone who had gotten close to the Turkish government summarized Erdogan's position on my case as "Why should we let him go when we have the Americans bending over backwards." It seemed that any goodwill gestures the US made, Erdogan assumed to be a surrender to his hardline stance. He just pocketed them and demanded more.

BEFORE LONG the media started repeating rumors that I would be indicted. While we were eating supper on March 13, Nejat noticed that the scrolling news feed at the bottom of the screen said my indictment had been submitted with a request for life in prison. My eyes were glued to the TV when the news anchor came on and, after listing my alleged crimes, confirmed that the prosecutor was demanding life in prison. My appetite was gone, and I just stood outside in the courtyard until the guards locked us in for the night. I went upstairs and read my psalm. "The LORD is on my side; I will not fear. What can man do to me?" I knew what the right answer was, but I was afraid. A life sentence will do that to you.

After this shock things went quiet. A couple of days later, Cem, my new lawyer, asked the prosecutor face-to-face if he had submitted an indictment. Karakaya's answer was a flat-out "No," until he paused and then dissembled a bit, muttering something along the lines of, "Well, maybe I sent a little something in." At the same time the embassy had sent a spokesperson to Izmir, because they thought there might be some movement leading to my release. I was in the dark about all of this until the morning of March 19, when a guard pushed a thick stack of papers through the metal slot in our door. "Sign this," he ordered. "This is your indictment."

They could have dropped my case. They could have sent me home. But they didn't.

I was going on trial.

PART SIX

19 | BACK TO THE PIT

THE 2018 ANNOUNCEMENT that Mike Pompeo was to be appointed secretary of state was a game changer. Not just because he promised to "put the swagger back in the State Department," or because he was a member of the same church denomination as Norine and I. Mike Pompeo's arrival was so significant for me because he sent us a message. "I am short on promises, long on action. Tell Andrew and Norine I am committed to action."

The process surrounding indictments is different in the US, where they are issued once a grand jury has reviewed the evidence supplied by a prosecutor and has agreed that there is enough of a case to go to trial. In Turkey the indictment is issued by the prosecutor without being reviewed by anyone. The prosecutor can make any accusations he wants and it is up to the court to then evaluate and decide to accept or dismiss the case.

This was a clear opportunity for Turkey to save face by having the judge review the charges against me and drop the case, or release me pending trial—and lift my travel restrictions—just like they had done with the German journalist. When Tillerson was still secretary of state, Turkish officials had discussed resolving my case. But within a week of his dismissal, they had moved ahead with the indictment, and the court had accepted it and decided to keep me in prison.

THE INDICTMENT was sixty-two pages long and full of ridiculous accusations. In the first pages I read that I was an agent of a shadowy organization called CAMA, which allegedly directs the CIA, NSA, FBI, and the American deep state, as well as all churches in the US. The accusations of one secret witness, code-named Dua, or "Prayer," took up almost half the indictment, and much of this was about the Mormons. It was all so bizarre that I could not believe what I was reading. According to Cem it was one of the sloppiest indictments he had ever seen.

It also surprised a few people in the State Department. Some US officials had at first thought I was simply caught up in the aftermath of the coup. With time they came to see that I was being held as a bargaining chip because of my nationality but were skeptical that it had anything to do with my faith. With the indictment out, it became clear that I had been targeted specifically because of my faith. My crime was "Christianization," acting as "an agent of unconventional and psychological warfare" under the "guise of an evangelical church pastor." All of our work was intended to fragment Turkey, they said, splitting it into pieces. Basically the indictment was associating "Christianization" with terrorism, and presenting Christianity as a danger to Turkey's unity.

When Karakaya had told me there were forty binders of material about me, he had not been bluffing. The media threw this number around to make it seem like there was a mountain of evidence, but as Cem and a dear church friend waded through the binders, they found that thirty-five of them had nothing to do with me—they were full of information about the Mormons. And much of the remaining five had no relevance to the case. But at least the files were now unsealed.

For the first time we learned that I had been kept in Sakran for eight months simply on the word of the secret witness, Dua. This man had earlier accused the Mormons in a court case but lost. On December 9—the day he sent me to prison—Karakaya called Dua in to make a new statement. Dua repeated the same accusations that had already been thrown out by the court, but this time he added, "Andrew was involved in all of that." Dua gave what he knew Karakaya wanted, and this was the "evidence" that the foreign minister had used to declare me a terrorist on TV right after the summit.

From the beginning, the Turks had kept changing the reason they gave for holding me, casting about for something that would stick. At first they were going to ban Norine and me from the country based on a request from the department combating human trafficking; then they decided to deport us as threats to national security. After a few weeks they told the State Department a new story—that I had gone to Syria to meet with the PKK. A couple of months later Karakaya accused me of making a speech praising Gulen in our church, and a week later, when the minister of justice met with Senator Lankford, he said I was under arrest because I had spoken negatively about Turkey to refugees, helped some of them leave Turkey, and attended a Gulen conference some years ago. None of these were true. But the pattern made sense.

It fit in with what a friend passed on to us from his talk with a Turkish governor early on in my imprisonment. Speaking about me, Erdogan had told the governor adamantly that they were not letting me go.

THE GOOD NEWS was that the charges that had been handed down to me by video the previous summer were gone, and I was no longer facing three life sentences. Either the TV reports from the previous week had been wrong, or the prosecutor had changed the indictment. But the charges leveled against me—military espionage as well as supporting FETO and the PKK—carried a potential sentence of thirty-five years. Since I'd turned fifty in January, it was as good as a life sentence.

My trial date was set for April, which gave me just under a month to work through the indictment and prepare my defense. It wasn't easy. I could not do even the most basic research because I was locked up, and I had limited time with Cem. Norine spent hours looking through the files, poring over phone records, emails, and messages, and gathering exculpatory evidence. This included going through my sermons in search of evidence that would help refute the claim that I had supported Kurdish separatists. She found a recording of me encouraging

183

Turks and Kurds to reconcile and "love one another," and another one in which I taught on the principle that Christians are to submit to our authorities and pray for them.

There were days when I worked with purpose, days when I felt inspired to press on and prepare my defense to the best of my abilities, glad for the opportunity to finally present the truth to the Turkish courts. Then there were days when I felt as though there was no point at all in my work. My fate was not in the hands of whatever Turkish judge heard my case. My fate was controlled by one man only—Erdogan. No judge was ever going to reach a verdict based on his own conclusions about me. They would only move when Erdogan told them to. My defense could be the best in the world, but it would make no difference.

I worked to remind myself that while President Erdogan did hold power in Turkey, the final word was always God's. And if God wanted me released from prison, then I'd be released. I just didn't know how, or when.

Now that my trial date was set, I noticed that I was being treated differently in Buca. Every time I met with Norine or Cem there were always twice as many guards around me, as well as an assistant prison director. My food delivery routine changed too. Until now Nejat and I had gotten our meals like everyone else, by handing out our cell's empty food bowls through the door's metal serving hatch to a fellow inmate who was supervised by a guard as he spooned out our allocation from the food cart and handed it back. But things changed after the indictment. A prison director would visit the kitchen and supervise our cell's food being taken out of a common pot and placed in sealed containers. He would then accompany the guards who walked the food to our cell and handed it directly to us.

The authorities clearly were not taking any chances with my security. According to reports in the Turkish media, the CIA was worried that I was about to reveal their secret plans for the region and were therefore preparing to assassinate me at any minute. It was almost funny, except that there were certain factions in Turkey that could want to create even more problems between the two countries. In the land of conspiracy theories, having a ready-made suspect would make it a whole lot easier if something happened to me.

ONE DAY I WAS READING in the Bible where Paul wrote, "Everyone looks out for their own interests, not those of Jesus Christ." I had read Philippians 2 many times, but this time this verse plunged straight into my heart. Paul was describing me! I was so caught up in my own concerns—gaining my freedom and returning to my family. But what about the interests of Jesus? What if his purposes were best served by my being kept in prison? I was sure that several years ago God had given me an assignment to prepare for a spiritual harvest in Turkey. Now as I heard about the large number of people praying for me around the world, and that it was not tapering off but actually spreading, I was beginning to see how it could serve God's interests for me to be in prison. I had become a magnet, drawing prayer into Turkey.

Should I not be willing to serve God by being in prison? I felt my failure so deeply. I wept and asked God to forgive me.

I GOT A REAL BOOST a couple of weeks before the trial when Senator Tillis, of my home state of North Carolina, visited me in prison. He told Norine, "I came to look him in the eye and assure him that he will not be forgotten." For a few months my hearing had been muffled and getting worse, so right before his visit I used a Q-tip to try to clean out my ears but ended up losing almost all my hearing. I had to cup my hands around my ears as Senator Tillis was forced to shout to me in the interview room. I could only hear faintly, but what he said came across loud and clear: "Let's wait and see what happens with this first trial date. If it does not go well, that is when we take the gloves off."

"THANK YOU, SENATOR!" I yelled as we said goodbye.

AS THE TRIAL APPROACHED, Cem told me what to expect. I had been scheduled to appear at the court on-site in Sakran, and we both assumed that I'd be driven there and back for each session. Cem reminded me that trial days in Turkey are spread out, often with months between each appearance. And while political trials can take five to ten years, he thought mine would be over in less than three years. I was terrified at the thought of being locked up for years on end while the trial dragged out.

Early Sunday morning, the day before my trial was due to begin, heavy banging on the door downstairs woke me up. Ramazan had been moved out some months earlier, so it was just Nejat and me in the cell now. A group of guards barged in, telling me to grab my things and get ready to go back to Sakran.

"Wait! My trial doesn't start until tomorrow."

"Yes. We're taking you there now. It's for your security—no one knows when we're moving you."

I really hadn't expected this. I barely had time to throw my notes, a few clothes, and other items into a bag. My fingers were fumbling, my head struggling to think straight. I hated Sakran so much that the thought of even being there for just one night was enough to set my heart racing and my throat closing up. And I was worried that it would be for much longer than one night. I kept trying to find out how long I would be there, but no one would tell me anything.

I'd been moved enough times that I thought I knew the routine, but as I waited to be taken outside to the courtyard things were different. There were dozens of military police standing around. I was given a bulletproof vest to put on before I stepped outside and into the bus, and we set off in a convoy.

I hated to think of leaving Buca. Everything about it had been better than Sakran. Nejat was the perfect cellmate who was happy to talk and happy to be silent. The place was quieter, cooler, and run in a more relaxed way. Even the food was better.

As soon as I arrived they processed me in—but not just as a visitor. This was a permanent transfer. I was here for the rest of my trial. Buca was over.

Right away I was placed in an isolation cell. The place was just as loud and chaotic as I remembered. I sat on the single bunk, spread out my trial notes and Bible beside me, and wept. I was back at Sakran, the place where I was considered a *hayvan*—an animal—and where I had felt my sanity and faith slipping away.

I still had work to do for the next day, but the thought of picking up a pen and getting down to it was just too much. I was devastated and overwhelmed.

I thought about Norine. My being in Sakran would be tough for her too. And our visits would be reduced to thirty-five minutes again. There would be no more letters in English, which meant that only Norine would be able to write to me. And I would be alone, in solitary confinement.

"Oh God," I called out. "You have brought me back to the place where I was crushed so badly. Why?"

He didn't reply. But someone else did.

"Hey," said a Turkish voice nearby. "New person in the cell next door. Who are you?"

At first I did not answer. But when he repeated his question a third time, I told him. "I'm the priest."

"Ah! I know you. I've been following your story."

20 | ON TRIAL

THE COURTROOM AT SAKRAN wasn't built to hold trials. It was built to host basketball matches. As I sat on my chair, my hands and legs shaking, staring up at the roof that towered above me, it seemed to me that almost everything about it was designed to throw me off balance and make me feel small.

I was sitting in an area that had been fenced off by a low wooden railing. Cem was way over on the side of the hall, so to communicate with him I had to get permission from the judge and then walk over accompanied by a couple of soldiers. Behind me, separated by a sea of what must have been five hundred empty seats, was the public gallery. If I turned around I could pick Norine out, but even straining my eyes, faces were a blur. When I first walked in the room Norine stood and waved so I would know where she was. In any case, Cem had told me not to look. "Keep your eyes to the front," he'd said. Most of the time I followed his advice, but when I turned to look at her, Norine would do what she could to encourage me—a hand over her heart meant "I love you and am with you," a thumbs-up told me "Well done!" and a finger pointing up told me to look to God.

The three judges were ten feet in front of me on a dais raised at least five or six feet high—so high that I had to tilt my head back to see. Next to them—right next to them on the dais itself—was the prosecutor.

On either side of them were two jumbo-sized video screens, each large enough for a movie theater.

I'd not been able to sleep at all the previous night, or the night before that. I hadn't eaten either, but the worst of it was that I had not been given my meds that morning. I was wired enough as it was without the sleep or the food, but without the Xanax my anxiety was in full flow. All I could think about was the fact that I was facing thirty-five years in prison and that even before it began everything about the trial was designed to find me guilty.

Cem had warned me that even though I was technically innocent until proven guilty, the fact that mine was a political crime meant that it was on me to prove my innocence. His words rang through my head as I listened to the judge open the trial with some preliminary business. The longer he spoke, the worse my shaking became.

Eventually the judge indicated that it was my turn to stand and address him.

When I spoke into the microphone, I was surprised that my voice was firm and strong. "Andrew Craig Brunson. I want to make my defense," I said, consulting the pages of handwritten notes that I had brought with me. The judge said nothing, and his two colleagues stared, stony-faced, at me. So I continued.

I went through every paragraph of the indictment, addressing every false claim and inaccuracy that the prosecutor had laid out against me. I stood perfectly still, my voice holding out, all the obscure Turkish legal words coming quickly to my mind, my hands and legs no longer shaking. Minutes went by and I carried on, explaining carefully and clearly why each and every accusation was groundless.

All through the morning I spoke, taking just the occasional sip from a bottle of water. The lead judge hardly ever looked at me or at my lawyer. Often when I looked up to check on him he'd be leaning over talking to one of the other judges, ignoring me completely. But I carried on. It was like I had a divine grace on me to speak clearly in spite of my panic, my trauma, and the lack of sleep, meds, and food.

When the three-hour mark was approaching, the judge interrupted and told me that it was time to break. The grace lifted and I panicked, suddenly drained of all the energy and focus that I'd had all morning. "Please," I begged the judge, "at the end of the day send me back to Buca." I was careful, because a director had warned me that very morning not to complain about the prison or the staff. "The problem isn't the prison, it's me—I have experienced a lot of trauma at Sakran."

The judge shrugged and said he'd consider it later, then waved at the two soldiers on either side to take me. They took me by the arms and pulled me along. The hall filled with noise as people went off for lunch, and I glanced helplessly at Norine as they took me into the holding cell.

The afternoon was harder than the morning. I spoke for a further three hours, then answered pointed questions about a text message that I'd sent to a pastor friend a few days after the coup. I had written that Turkey was being shaken—by the coup, and also the after-coup purges and acceleration toward one-man rule—but that this hardship would result in many people turning to Jesus: "I think things will become darker, and we will also see breakthrough in glory and miracles. We win in the end." The judge insisted this was proof that I had helped to plan the coup.

I tried to be clear in my defense, telling the judge that I had preached for many years that God allows the things we trust in to be shaken, so that we will turn to him. The judge did not seem at all impressed.

THEN IT WAS MY TURN to listen as three witnesses testified. Before each spoke they were sworn in by the flamboyant clerk of the court, who directed everyone present to stand and follow his lead as he puffed out his chest and pompously held his hand over his heart, his head tilted back, gazing with the look of a true believer into the distance, proud to be a part of Turkish justice in action as each false witness took his solemn oath. And while it made me want to laugh, the sight of the secret witnesses giving their testimony from another location and appearing like big brother on the two screens that loomed overhead disgusted me and made me angry. This was a cynical game. There was no good reason to keep them secret since there was no security risk for them. In fact, we knew their identity in each case, but because it is a crime to say who they are, we were kept from exposing their motivations and lies. And the judge told them that as secret witnesses they did not have to answer any questions they did not want to.

All the witnesses, the ones who hid their identity and the ones who did not, lied.

The one code-named Dua spun a long story about how he had heard me teach that the Kurds were the thirteenth lost tribe of Israel, and I was actively working to dismember Turkey to set up a Christian state for them. I had never heard of a thirteenth tribe, let alone preached it, but Dua confidently asserted that all Christians teach this, and that I shared this idea with the Mormons, and in fact that I was the leader of a Mormon church.

I couldn't believe it when the judge solemnly asked Dua to explain more about CAMA, the crazy conspiracy theory he had detailed in the indictment. Dua assured the judge that all pastors in Turkey were agents of the American deep state sent to break up Turkey. It all sounded like a James Bond movie, and I wanted to laugh. But the judges and prosecutor were not laughing. They were listening intently.

DUA WASN'T DONE. He had plenty more to say about me. According to him I had gathered information about people working on the railroads to prepare for an invasion of Turkey, and this proved I was a military spy. Apart from never having seen any of this before, I asked the judge whether the names of railroad employees were even classified to begin with. The judge said, "*We* will determine what is a state secret." Cem pulled out a thick stack of printouts and slapped it down on the table in front of him as he asked to submit some evidence to the court. The judge reluctantly nodded for the clerk to take it. It was a list of all the employees of the state railroad, an even longer one than Dua had given. "I googled these and downloaded them from the internet," announced Cem. "Anybody can do this. How can you say this is secret information?" The judge was silent, clearly unhappy.

I watched the blurred outline of Dua's face and listened to his digitally distorted voice—a low growl like some kind of horror movie—as he went on for several hours. I wanted to stand up and shout that he was a fraud. I knew that he'd been kicked out of a church for swindling people. He told the judge, "Brunson baptized twenty-five people, took their money, and told them he could help get them to Canada." Actually, this was just one of the tricks *he* had pulled. I knew that he'd then worked as a translator for the Mormons before they kicked him out. That was when he'd opened a court case against them, but lost, and it was those same accusations that had failed against the Mormons that he was now recycling against me. But my hands were tied. The prosecutor would open a new court case against me if I exposed who he was. So I sat in silence and prayed that the truth would somehow come out.

The next secret witness we knew very well. She had caused all kinds of problems in the short time she was in our church and had left threatening, "Just wait and see what I do to you." It had made us feel sick to learn that she was an actual witch, deeply involved in the occult.

More than once the judge berated me for not following correct protocol—like not responding to a witness with a statement or not approaching the podium when he addressed me. It was exhausting, and by the time he brought the trial to a conclusion it was getting close to ten at night.

"The next date for this trial is May 7. You will remain in prison." I begged the judge to return me to Buca. He said he would recommend a move, but added that he could not make that decision. Two military police officers grabbed my arms and led me toward the prisoner exit. "Norine!" I shouted, struggling to see her in the crowd at the back of the hall. "Get me out of here! I'm going crazy!" Senator Tillis had come, along with Sam Brownback, Ambassador-at-Large for International Religious Freedom, and other friends from various churches were present. I was nearly at the door, but I was so grateful for their support. I knew some had come just to pray me through. I filled my lungs for one final shout: "Thank you to all who came!"

Minutes later, I was back in my cell in Sakran. Alone.

SENATOR TILLIS'S REACTION to what he'd seen in court that Monday was instant and strong. In the trial I had been accused of having a secret room in the church where secret meetings took place around a secret map that showed how I was planning on dividing up the country for the Kurds. Several witnesses testified to seeing this room and described PKK flags hanging on the walls and other propaganda material around the church. On the Tuesday, Senator Tillis asked Norine to show him around the church so that he could see this secret room for himself. It was just our small church office. By Friday, a bipartisan group of sixty-six senators led by Senators Tillis and Jeanne Shaheen had sent a letter to Erdogan demanding my release. The letter called my indictment "an absurd collection of anonymous accusations, flights of fantasy, and random character assassination. . . . It is an insult not only to an unjustly imprisoned individual, but to the traditions of Turkish jurisprudence."

As for me, for a third night running I couldn't sleep. I had no appetite and could do nothing but lie on my bed, feeling crushed. For months I had been winning small victories at Buca, but now I had been knocked down again. I was ready to give up.

Even the guards appeared to be concerned about me. "Come, come," said the head guard the day after the trial—a man who had previously been harsh with me when I'd been in my old cell. "I'll help you outside. It'll be good for you to get some air. Come."

Finally I gave in, but after ten minutes in the courtyard I asked to go back inside. Even without the trial the thought of being stuck in Sakran again was too much.

The head guard took me back and left me. I lay there alone, fearful, and with terrible grief pouring down my cheeks. The thoughts kept going through my mind: *Where are you, God? Why have you let them return me to this awful place? Why have you not intervened for me? Why are you so far away, so silent?*

I opened my mouth, weeping aloud, and the words I heard murmured stunned me: "I love you, Jesus!"

And again, "I love you, Jesus! I love you, Jesus!"

Immediately I realized, *Here is my victory!* In my lowest point the cry of my heart was one of love to Jesus. I was elated. This was a triumph in my heart, a response to God that showed me how different things were for me now. When I was in Sakran before I had been so full of fear and pain. I still had fear and pain, but I had just discovered how deep my devotion was. It had been tried and proven true.

EVEN THOUGH I WAS IN A SOLITARY CELL, there was some contact with other inmates. I couldn't see them, but if we raised our voices I could talk to the men in the cells on either side of mine through the window, and whenever someone was walking in the courtyard it was possible to talk to him too. That's how I discovered that the people around me were military men who had been charged with playing a major part in the attempted coup. Of the few I met briefly, two were generals and the others were elite soldiers. Whatever lies and charges I was facing, I was sure that their prospects were far worse than mine.

It was one of the generals who had first spoken to me when I arrived the night before my trial. Now a second general encouraged me. "Be strong," he said. "Be strong. When I was brought in here I wanted to die too. I wanted to give up. But I became strong and the same will happen to you. And besides, I've been watching your case. They're going to let you out in the next trial."

I wasn't sure that he was right about the release, but I drew comfort from his thoughtfulness. And one of my neighbors showed his kindness in another way. Through the bars of his window he dropped a cold Coke and a bowl to eat from to a prisoner taking his one hour in the courtyard, who then lobbed it up to my window. He also passed on some encouraging news he had heard on TV. The day after my trial

President Trump had tweeted that I was being persecuted in Turkey for no reason: "They call him a spy, but I am more a spy than he is."

"It's going to be all right," said the man standing in the courtyard. "Don't worry. It's all going to work out."

"Go ahead," said the general, "tell the priest what you're in for."

The man laughed. "I was on the team that's accused of being the assassination squad. But we were just told at the last minute that we needed to go to a certain hotel in the city. We didn't even have an address, and we had to stop at a local store to ask for directions. Does that sound like the way an elite squad would go about assassinating a president?"

What could I say? I knew he was in a world of trouble.

Their encouragement and perspective really touched me. I couldn't believe that men who were facing life in solitary confinement were trying to lift my spirits.

LATER, WHEN I WAS TAKEN to see the prison psychologist, as all new intakes must, things went sour again.

"Andrew, we're going to take good care of you. So you're going to stay here for a few months, maybe a few years, but you'll be fine here."

I broke down. "Please just ask them to send me back!"

She paused. "Okay. I'll ask." But I knew she couldn't do much.

I slumped back to my cell. I had hope that between Norine, the embassy, and some of our friends in the US government that I would be moved. But how long would it take? And there were no guarantees. They could keep me here just to increase the pressure. I settled in to wait.

But I didn't have to wait long. On the fifth day, two guards opened my cell door and told me that they were sending me back to Buca.

"Really? When?"

"Now."

I gathered the handful of clothes, my trial notes, and my Bible and was ready to go within minutes. I managed a smile at the guard as I thanked him.

He quickly waved my words away. "Honestly, we're all breathing a sigh of relief that you're going."

I never thought I could be happy to go to prison, but it was such a relief to return to my cell in Buca. Nejat was pleased to see me and greeted me like I had never been away.

21 | FALSE WITNESSES

THREE WEEKS AFTER I FIRST SAT IN THE BASKETBALL COURT, I stood near the entrance to Buca Prison and got ready to run. I was heading back for my second trial day, and security was tighter than before. I'd already been strip-searched, cuffed, and strapped into a bulletproof vest, but there was more to come. I was surrounded by several armed military police, and as soon as one of their radios told them to go, they ran me out across a parking lot into the prisoner transport bus. I couldn't see through the blacked-out window, and I sat quietly in the secure cubicle in the bus. The engine was already running, but for almost a minute we just sat there, me and my blank-faced soldiers with their machine guns at the ready.

Another message came through the radio. One of the men jumped up and pulled me out of the bus and onto an identical one which had just arrived in the courtyard. The decoy bus drove off without me, and we waited for our turn to leave, escorted by several police cars.

When we arrived at Sakran, the short walk from the transport bus to the court's prisoner entrance was flanked by twenty or more commandos. The soldiers guarding me crowded around in a tight cluster and jogged me through the tunnel that the commandos formed, their arms tight on mine.

None of this was for show. The trial had made me a target, a hate figure even. I don't think they were especially concerned that US forces might fly in by helicopter and rescue me. They were guarding me from their own people.

I KNEW that it was going to be a difficult day. Three witnesses had testified against me on the first day, but there were seven lined up for this second trial day, two of them in secret. As the judges arrived and took up their position on the dais, I braced myself for the lies to begin.

I glanced back and was touched to see the pastor from our family's church in North Carolina standing next to Norine. It was a reminder that fastings and prayer vigils were going on in countless places.

The first witness was secret, but I knew who he was although I had never met him. For a few months, he'd attended a church we started in another city, but the leadership there had asked him to leave when he caused serious problems. He claimed that I gave coordinates to the US military to drop weapons to the PKK, that I was bringing PKK fighters to Izmir for medical treatment and that I was a leader in FETO. After him another secret witness told how she'd seen a message on someone's phone warning to prepare for an earthquake—evidence, the prosecutor said, of my involvement in the coup. But she said she didn't know me, and that the message wasn't from me, so I was puzzled what the connection was. After her there were no more secret witnesses, but they were all just as ridiculous.

A convict, who appeared to be mentally ill, took the stand and declared that I was the leader of the Jehovah's Witnesses, and together with them had helped plan the Gezi Park protests that had swept the country back in 2013. Erdogan was now calling these an attempt to overthrow his government. And after him there came another convict who was obviously hoping to see his sentence cut by spreading more lies about me.

"Andrew Brunson worked for the Fethullah Gulen organization, his church was funded by them, and he knew a bunch of the main leaders. I also saw him meeting with members of the PKK terrorist group in the Hilton Hotel in Gaziantep."

"Really?" said the judge, leaning in. "And did you ever see Andrew Brunson with Murat Safa?"

"Yes, yes I did, sir."

"You did!" said the judge, clapping his hands and smiling. "And did you ever see him with Bekir Baz?"

"Yes."

Another clap and a smile. "And Enver Muslim? Did you see Andrew Brunson with him?"

"Oh yes. I definitely saw him with all of these people."

Before Cem asked the witness some questions I stood up to make my statement. "Your Honor, I never met with any of the people he mentioned. I've never even been to that hotel. And you have my phone records that prove I didn't visit Gaziantep that year." I added with exasperation, "And you're feeding him all these names and he's saying yes to every one of them. If you give him ten more names he'll say yes to those as well."

The judge just stared at me.

When Cem stood he looked directly at the witness. "Have you ever been to prison before this?"

The man froze for a second, then scratched his chin and stared up at the ceiling. "Well, I was in prison once before. Or maybe twice. Or . . . let me think . . . maybe three times?"

Cem turned to the judge. "I want to present to the court evidence that this man has been convicted fourteen times for fraud and there are twenty-four other outstanding warrants for his arrest."

I wanted to jump up and shout for joy, but the judge stared at the piece of paper that Cem had just handed him. "How is this relevant?"

I was flabbergasted, and so was Cem. "He's a fraud, Your Honor. How can it not be relevant?"

The judge wasn't listening. Everyone was following orders from Ankara, but many of them had their own attitudes as well. He was showing his true colors.

THE NEXT WITNESS claimed to have been a friend of mine for years, though I'd never met him in my life. He described concerts we hosted where we sang songs about the PKK, waved terrorist flags, and gave speeches about the PKK.

Years earlier, after I had been attacked by the gunman in the street, I'd been assigned a couple of bodyguards by the Counter-Terror Police. I stopped using the bodyguards after a couple of weeks, but they told me something that didn't surprise me at all at the time: "We have a thick file on you. The government has been monitoring you for years." Cem had somehow also been able to get a report from MIT (the National Intelligence Agency) acknowledging that they keep track of all foreigners they think may be missionaries.

Armed with these facts, I stood up and addressed the court.

"I have been accused of so many things, from running PKK rallies and concerts to military spying and coordinating the transfer of weapons, and yet it is clear that for years I have been followed by MIT and Counter-Terror. So how could I have carried out all these crimes while your own government agencies have had me under close watch? If I had done any of these things wouldn't there be some concrete, physical proof? And yet you've found no texts, or emails. There are no phone records linking me to anybody. There are no sound clips of me preaching these messages, no video or pictures of the church supposedly full of propaganda and PKK flags. Our church is on a busy street, the windows and doors are always open. How could terrorist activity go on in the open for years and no one ever report it? The reason is because none of it ever happened. Why don't your witnesses provide any supporting evidence? How can you listen to them when they have no proof?"

The judge leaned back in his chair. "They don't have to provide any evidence to support what they're saying. Their testimony is evidence."

I was dumbfounded. "How can this be? How can I defend myself when all they have to do is assert something and you accept it? This doesn't make sense."

The judge answered sharply, "I'm not going to argue with you."

THE DAY WAS LONG, and by the time it drew to a close I was exhausted. I still had a faint hope as the judge looked down at me and asked me what I wanted to happen next, but I knew it was a hollow formality, a routine question that he had to ask at the end of every day of trial.

Even so, I told him exactly what I wanted. "I just want to go home, Your Honor."

If he listened to me at all, it didn't make any difference. With his final words he told me that I would remain in custody and that my next hearing was scheduled for July 18, two and a half months away.

On the way back to Buca I cried tears of anger and frustration.

22 | THE HOSTAGE

I WAS ANGRY. The second day of trial had been such a farce that I didn't feel any motivation to prepare for the third. Was there even any point in making a defense? I was fed up with the Turkish government and its public posturing, putting on a righteous front, and insisting that their judiciary was independent when behind the scenes they had been haggling for me like a trader in a bazaar. Even my next trial date was political, pushing my case off until after the election that Erdogan had just called, so that he could look strong by standing up to the US. There would be media there, as well as representatives from the US, and it seemed to me that the third trial date was a good opportunity to hit back and call it what it was: a kangaroo court.

Then again, maybe I'd refuse to go at all. If I withdrew completely I would not have to sit through any more of the charade. But if I didn't show up, how else would I get the truth on the record?

My bad mood following the second day of trial was lifted by two special visits. The first was a wonderful surprise visit from my son Blaise. He was standing off to the side as I walked in to meet Norine, and even as I hugged him it took me a few moments to get my head around the fact that he was actually there in person with me. My open visit just happened to coincide with Father's Day.

The second visit was also unexpected.

Visits never happened at the weekend, but one Saturday I was taken into the room where I had met with Blaise and Jacqueline almost a year earlier—the one with the padded walls that allowed them to record the audio more accurately—and introduced to Senator Shaheen and Senator Lindsey Graham.

They'd met with Erdogan the day before and Senator Shaheen had told him that the US knew that the witnesses testifying against me were lying. Erdogan acknowledged to Senator Shaheen that there were indeed problems with the witnesses, and even suggested that the main secret witness might himself be a Gulenist who was leading officials astray on my case. By reframing this as a Gulenist plot he was backtracking, showing signs that he was looking for a way out of the corner he had boxed himself into. Erdogan was softer and more relaxed than they expected and agreed to their request to visit me. "He would not have met with us to talk about this, or given permission for us to see you, if there wasn't thought of some movement on your case," said Senator Graham. Very soon after this meeting Norine received word that the two presidents had talked, and Erdogan again admitted that there was a problem with the credibility of the witnesses.

There was another reason for their visit. They had a message for me.

"You are a hostage," said Senator Graham. "The US will not make deals for hostages. We are going to get you out of here, but it has to be in the right way. You have to be patient. So hang on, Andrew."

I told them both that I understood. I knew that most mission organizations have a policy that they won't pay ransoms, because if they did it would put a target on the backs of all their workers. I agreed with the policy, and I did not want my release to put anyone else at risk. But it was still hard to hear.

But I also understood this was a message to Erdogan. There was no doubt at all that our conversation was being recorded. I knew it, and the senators knew it as well. The message would be reported back to Erdogan: the US would not trade for me.

When our time was almost up, I remembered that Senator Graham was a good friend of Senator John McCain, who was undergoing treatment for cancer at the time. "My uncle was a POW in Vietnam," I said. "He was held in the same prison as Senator McCain. I've always admired the way McCain was willing to remain there to avoid becoming a propaganda coup. That took a lot of courage."

AS THE THIRD TRIAL DATE APPROACHED, relations between the US and Turkey appeared to be improving. With the US scaling down operations in Syria, the news was full of reports about the proposal to hand over patrols in the Syrian town of Manbij to Turkish forces. The plan was for three months of joint patrols followed by a full handover, but I knew that my case was part of the agreement and the handover was conditional. This was a significant carrot for Turkey, which was desperate to get access to Manbij and flush out the Kurdish troops living there. From time to time the Turkish media announced that the joint patrols had begun, which demoralized me. But every time that happened Norine would remind me at our next visit not to believe everything I saw on TV.

There were other reasons to be optimistic as well. CeCe had made sure that the State Department knew the facts about my case. So when Secretary Pompeo met with his Turkish counterpart after my second trial day and was told "there is nothing we can do," he called the foreign minister on it.

"But you do have the power to intervene," said Secretary Pompeo, referring him to Decree 694, Article 74 from the previous summer. "The President has the power to return prisoners to their home countries." This silenced the foreign minister. After this he did not make the same excuse again, although people under him continued to.

ON THE DAY OF THE HEARING, I sat in my usual seat, dwarfed by the dais and the jumbotron video screens, and listened to the first witness, Levent, lie about me. I knew him, and I knew that all his lies came from bitterness because he had not been given a position of leadership

207

in our church. And when it was my turn to stand before the judges and deliver my response, I knew exactly what I wanted to say.

Throughout the weeks leading up to the third trial date I had decided that I would use it as an opportunity to share my faith. Although I couldn't control what others did, and there was no point in trying to establish logic or reason in the court, I could at least choose what I would say and how I would say it. I wanted to take a stand as a representative of Jesus Christ, without apology or shame.

I stood in front of the microphone and listened to my opening words echo around the hall. "The most important thing in my life is my faith." I had decided that even though I was in court, I was going to preach.

> Jesus told his disciples to go into all the world and proclaim the good news of salvation to everyone and make disciples. This is why I came to Turkey—to proclaim this.
>
> There is only one way to God: Jesus.
>
> There is only one way to have our sins forgiven: Jesus.
>
> There is only one way to gain eternal life: Jesus.
>
> There is only one Savior: Jesus.
>
> I want this to echo in all of Turkey.
>
> Many lies have been said about me in the media—that I am a FETO terrorist, a member of the PKK terror group, a CIA agent. But what I would like people to know about me is this: for the last twenty-five years I have declared Jesus as Savior! For twenty-three years I did it by choice, and the last two years I have been forced to do it from prison, but my message is the same.
>
> The Bible says to forgive one another "as God in Christ forgave you." And in another place it says, "Bless those who persecute you; bless and do not curse." And so, I forgive those who have wronged me, who have caused me harm, who have lied about me, who have borne false witness against me. I forgive each and every witness. I forgive Levent.

I went on to name each witness, one by one. I wanted to state that I forgive Erdogan, Cavusoglu, and the others who were really keeping me there—because I did. But I could not say that in court. I ended with these words: "I will hold no hatred against them in my heart, and I leave them to God. May God have mercy."

As soon as I finished, the judge quickly called the next two witnesses. There were more lies said about me, but I stayed calm, glad that I'd made my statement and looking forward to the time when we would be allowed to call our first witness.

We had a lineup of strong witnesses who could completely expose and discredit the ones against me, but so far the judge was only allowing one to testify. Even so, I thought Deniz was an important witness because as the president of our church board he was actually legally responsible for everything that went on there.

Deniz took his seat to the side of the dais and listened carefully to Cem describe the accusations that various witnesses had made against me. He described PKK flags, sermons in support of Gulen, secret meetings, and hidden agendas to divide up the country.

"None of this happened," said Deniz calmly but emphatically. "I never saw anything like what you describe."

When it was the judge's turn to interrogate Deniz, he waved his hand and said he had no questions. The prosecutor also had nothing to ask, so it went back to the judge.

The judge stared at Cem. "If this is how the rest of your witnesses are going to testify then there's no reason for us to listen to them. If there is a murder and someone witnesses it, we want to hear from him. We don't need to talk to all the people who didn't see it. Your witness says he hasn't seen any of the things the other witnesses have, so of what use is he? Why should we listen to him?"

I was disgusted. This was completely illogical. I wanted to stand up and shout, but Cem motioned me to let it go for now.

As soon as Deniz was dismissed, one of the junior judges leaned over and said something to the main judge. He looked instantly alert and immediately started running through the usual procedural items that always came at the end of the trial, though I had no idea why.

Cem was looking puzzled too, and the whole room was alive with energy.

The judge asked me what my request was regarding continuing imprisonment, which was usually one of the final pieces of business in the trial day. I stood up and pleaded, "Please, Your Honor, I have waited two and a half months for this trial session. I would like to make my defense and respond to the witnesses."

He shook his head. "Send it in writing or give it to your lawyer. I need to know what your request is now, we're finishing for the day." He was moving quickly to shut things down but I was intent on making one more statement. Risking his anger, I plunged in quickly.

After I was arrested I was able to meet with my mother and she said to me, "From the time of Jesus until now, Jesus's disciples have suffered for his sake. There is a long line going all the way back—a line that stretches two thousand years. My son, it is now your turn to stand in that line." I am innocent of all these charges brought against me. But I know why I am really here: For the sake of Jesus Christ I have been given the privilege not only of believing in him, but also of suffering for his sake. I was appointed to proclaim Jesus's death and resurrection. This is the reason why I am suffering. But I am not ashamed.

Jesus said, "Blessed are you when people insult you, persecute you and falsely say all kinds of evil against you because of me. Rejoice and be glad, because great is your reward in heaven, for in the same way they persecuted the prophets who were before you."

The judge interrupted impatiently. "Are you almost done?"
"One more minute, please!" I continued:

I have been given an assignment—to be imprisoned for the sake of Jesus. This is a very difficult thing, to be separated from my children, separated from my wife. It has been twenty-two months now. But I bear this assignment, for the sake of Jesus. And I declare—
Blessed am I, because for the sake of Jesus many people have wronged me, have persecuted me, and I am now suffering.

Blessed am I, because I have been forcibly separated from my wife and children.

Blessed am I, because every kind of lie has been told about me, because all kinds of slander has been said about me.

Blessed am I, because I am in prison.

I am kept in prison by force, I do not want to be there. But I choose willingly to suffer for the sake of Jesus, and by suffering for his sake I hope to display for everyone his incomparable worth.

And I want Turkey to know—it is for his sake that I am here.

I sat down. I felt defiant. The Turkish government had set out to crush me, to trash my ministry and break my faith and intimidate other Christians from speaking out. I knew there was still a lot they could do to hurt me. But at that moment I was holding my head high. It was a holy defiance. *Was this what David felt when he went against Goliath?*

The judge frowned. "You're going back to prison. Next court date in three months."

And with that, the hall erupted with noise as a soldier on each side of me locked his arms with mine and steered me out.

THE NIGHT BEFORE the third trial date the chargé d'affaires had told Norine, "If this doesn't do it, I don't know what will." Whatever he had expected, it hadn't worked. He left the trial looking shocked and went to make phone calls.

By God's grace the next day was Thursday, my weekly visiting day. Norine and I were both discouraged that the next hearing was so far out. She sounded particularly weighed down by it all, although she did have some good news. "President Trump tweeted about you. He said you'd been held hostage for far too long and that you'd done nothing wrong."

"That's good," I said. "Calling me a hostage publicly makes it clear that the government believes in my innocence." It also meant that the US did not accept the judicial procedure as legitimate.

By the time of our biweekly phone call the next day, Norine had some more news for me. "They had a deal. There was a plane waiting for you. The Turks backed out." Norine went on, "Senator Graham called me. He said that two days ago it was looking good, yesterday not so good. But we should give it a week and see what happens."

I was encouraged by the news, but there had been deals in the past, and I was still in prison.

That weekend I read something in my Bible that struck me and resonated in my mind for days.

It was a passage telling what happened the night that Jesus was arrested. Peter pulled out his sword to save Jesus, but Jesus told him to put his sword away. "Shall I not drink the cup the Father has given me?"

Late on Tuesday evening, six days after the third trial date, I sat on my bed and wrote to Norine.

> *This sentence keeps resonating in my mind as I go through the daily—sometimes hourly—struggle of submitting myself— beyond that, of intentionally embracing—whatever God's plans are that have allowed for ongoing imprisonment. "Shall I not drink the cup?" I want to "drink the cup" faithfully, to the dregs. But then I also say, "Lord, I've been drinking this cup for close to two years. How much longer?" But, may I be faithful to the end. May I be willing to drink the cup—continue drinking it . . . How could I do otherwise? At my best I am at that point. And then I quail with fear, I don't want to go on day after day. And yet, I want to be an obedient son.*

The next morning I read through the letter again, sealed it, and handed it to the guard who came for roll call. A little over a year earlier I had arrived at Buca a broken man. But God had been rebuilding me.

That afternoon I was in the courtyard when I heard someone calling for me at the metal serving hatch in the cell door. I walked over, knelt down, and looked up to see the prison director. That was unusual.

"Andrew, what's your address here in Izmir?"

"What do you want it for?"

"You'll see."

I told him.

A few minutes later it was Nejat's turn to call my name. "Uh, Andrew? You really need to come and see what's on the TV."

"Why?"

"Just come here, Andrew. Now!"

PART SEVEN

23 | BROKEN DEAL

I FOLLOWED NEJAT'S FINGER POINTING TO the ticker running across the bottom of the screen. "Priest Brunson released to house arrest for health reasons."

It was the last thing I expected. Over the twenty-two months I had been locked away I had thought a lot about how they might let me go. Maybe they'd take me directly to the airport from the prison, or perhaps they'd stash me away in a deportation center like Harmandali first. But house arrest? That had never even crossed my mind. And what health reasons were they referring to? I was confused.

The prison director came into the cell, a handful of guards behind him. "Andrew, you've been released to house arrest. Gather your things."

I didn't say anything. No questions, no queries. I was too busy throwing everything that I wanted to take with me into trash bags. The pile of items that I was leaving grew ever larger. When I was done I grabbed my guitar and turned to Nejat, pointing at the collection of tuna cans, toothpaste, blank notepads, and pens that I was leaving. "All these things I leave to you." We hugged at the door.

"Any offenses against me, do you release them?" He knew we would probably never see each other again, and like any good Muslim Nejat felt the need to end on good terms, or face paying for any offenses on judgment day.

I smiled at him. "Yes, of course, my friend." There was nothing to forgive. The only debt between us was a debt of gratitude for all the encouragement and kindness he had shown me. We hugged again and I felt deeply sad that this good man and father of three was being left imprisoned unjustly.

As I followed the director downstairs the place was buzzing. Phones were ringing and people were hurrying. "Where's your wife?" the director asked me at one point. "She's not answering her phone."

I had no idea where she was. I had no idea about anything. It was all so surreal. Thirty minutes earlier I had been pacing in the courtyard, praying. I'd woken up with the same familiar fear and dull terror that greeted me every morning, and I was midway through my daily battle to surrender.

After I'd been officially processed out and had my passport, IDs, and money returned to me, I was bustled outside. For the first time I was not handcuffed. There was no bulletproof vest to wear and no decoy bus ready to leave without me. There was just me, a pile of my clothes and books and—most importantly—my letters in trashbags, and several police officers around me, waiting for someone to tell them what to do next.

"Wait!" I remembered the letter I'd written to Norine. It had felt so significant as I wrote it, and I wanted to take it with me. Now that my prison account was closed they would not mail it on, so one of the prison directors was kind enough to send a guard to look for it in the mailroom.

The waiting continued and I stood quietly while people came and went. Several police cars lined up, and my belongings were loaded into one of them. When the main gates opened I could see a crowd of media gathered outside. A guard ran up to me and handed me my letter to Norine.

"Thank you," I said, holding it close. Whatever was coming next I wanted to remember the place of surrender that I'd reached in Buca.

EVERY SINGLE MAJOR NEWS OUTLET appeared to have heard about my release and sent a vehicle to trail our convoy. There was too much to process, and as soon as someone told me that they'd heard from Norine and that she was also part of the traffic flowing behind us, I closed my eyes. Soon I'd be home again with my wife. That was all that really mattered.

When we finally pulled up outside our apartment in Izmir the police had closed off our narrow street. That hadn't stopped people crowding around the barriers though, and we waited in the car until Norine called to say that she was inside the apartment. There had been a small logistical problem—I didn't have my keys anymore, so we had to wait for her to arrive. As soon as I stepped out of the car, I was swarmed.

All the noise, the camera, and the faces trying to press close and break through the guards who surrounded me—it was chaotic. After spending so long seeing the same few faces day in and day out, this felt intense. I could see some of my friends from church in the crowd—singing and celebrating. I was very emotional—the last time I had been here was when I got up from breakfast and innocently walked out the door to visit the police station almost twenty-two months ago. I had been sure I would never step foot in my apartment again. As the police walked me up the stairs I caught sight of Norine. She was waiting on the small stairwell landing in front of our flat, but when she saw me she launched herself down the stairs and threw her arms around my neck. This was an impossible dream come true.

The police officers hurried us inside. As soon as we were in, Norine and I got down on our knees in the living room, embraced each other, and prayed. "Thank you, God. Thank you. Thank you."

The six officers stayed with us for a couple of hours. They set up the monitoring box and fitted me with an ankle bracelet, telling me not to take it off or leave the apartment. There was a constant buzz of noise from the street outside and so many people asking to see us, but the police told us they wouldn't allow any visitors that night. "Just be quiet here tonight, okay?"

It was fine by me. I hadn't spoken to Jordan, our eldest son, since the arrest, and I was desperate to call. As soon as I saw his face on my phone,

I wept. I couldn't say a word for five minutes. We must have spent a few hours on the phone talking with Jacqueline, Blaise, and my parents.

Norine put on a worship song. For twenty-two months this kind of music had been torn from my world. I'd heard plenty of Turkish music in prison, but nothing that spoke to me of God's love and care. As the sound filled me from the inside out, I lay on our bed, overcome with emotion.

Suddenly I remembered the letter that I'd finished the day before. It was crumpled from being in my pocket, but as I handed it to Norine I tried to explain why it was so important. "You know how I struggled, how low I went, how broken I was? I wrote this last night, not knowing I was about to be released. It says 'I am willing to drink the cup, to the dregs.' I want you to know how I finished at Buca. I finished in victory. Norine, by the grace of God I ended well."

THE NEXT DAY WAS JUST AS STRANGE. I woke up in my own bed, next to my wife, not to the sound of guards doing roll call, but of police talking on the street below our window. I was no longer in prison, but I was still far from being free. We could not fully rejoice because house arrest was not enough—it needed to go to a full release, and we had no guarantee of that. We were delighted, but apprehensive.

The news of my release to house arrest was big in the Turkish media. Every news site I visited or TV channel I flicked on to was carrying the story. And as the day wore on I gained a clearer understanding of why I'd been released.

In the course of their discussions, Erdogan had asked President Trump to secure the release of a Turkish citizen who had been detained in another Middle Eastern country. Trump had helped and the individual in question arrived back in Turkey on July 15, three days before my third trial day. There had been other discussions about the Turkish banker, now convicted in the US of violating the embargo against Iran, and there was an agreement that if I was released he would be allowed to serve the rest of his sentence at home. But at the last minute, when an agreement was already in place, the Turks broke the deal by drastically increasing their demands, asking that the US investigation into the state bank Halkbank—which was likely to result in billions of dollars in fines—be dropped completely before releasing me. Trump had gotten angry at Erdogan, banging his desk while on the phone and yelling at him, "We had a deal!"

This explained the abrupt stop to my third trial session, and why the judge's demeanor suddenly changed and he quickly wrapped things up. He must have been told that the deal was off and that I was to be returned to Buca.

My release to house arrest was Erdogan's way of trying to backtrack, and the Turkish media presented it as a simple communication problem. The way they told it, President Trump thought that Erdogan had said I would be going home to the US, when in fact Erdogan meant home to house arrest in Izmir.

It was the last straw, and on my first full day at home President Trump took to Twitter to make the US position clear: "The United States will impose large sanctions on Turkey for their long time detainment of Pastor Andrew Brunson, a great Christian, family man and wonderful human being. He is suffering greatly. This innocent man of faith should be released immediately!"

President Trump wasn't the only US politician making the Turkish news that day. Vice President Pence addressed Erdogan directly in a speech, telling him: "To President Erdogan and the Turkish government, I have a message on behalf of the president of the United States of America. Release Pastor Andrew Brunson now, or be prepared to face the consequences. If Turkey does not take immediate action to free this innocent man of faith and send him home to America, the United States will impose significant sanctions on Turkey until Pastor Andrew Brunson is free."

The message could not have been more clear: if Turkey did not release me, sanctions were coming.

The response from the Turkish media was equally clear: I should be sent back to prison straightaway. This was really frightening.

Things were chaotic, but there was a feeling that something could happen soon, even over the weekend.

Very late the next night, a former US ambassador came to visit us. He had made contact through mutual friends, and we were led to believe he was in some way involved in brokering a deal between the governments.

We googled him and confirmed that he was an American, and had been an ambassador years ago. But even though he wanted my situation to be resolved, it did not take long before we realized that it was not my government's interests he was representing. It was Turkey's.

He wanted to talk about the threat of sanctions. "This isn't the way to do things," he said. "This is a mistake and you need to get to Trump and tell him to back off."

Norine and I looked at each other. "Well," I said, standing up and walking him to the door. "I'm not going to do that. I don't tell the president what to do. I certainly wish no harm on the Turkish people, but I don't believe this will be resolved without some action by the US. Erdogan has had many opportunities to make this right but has chosen not to."

THE NEXT DAY CAME AND WENT. The weekend slipped by. "Be ready to go," we were told. "A week, maybe ten days." We took the advice and started to pack our clothes, cautiously hopeful that we would soon be leaving Turkey behind us.

The ten-day mark approached, and I was still trapped inside the apartment, still wearing the ankle bracelet, still looking out onto the street to see police officers guarding me. And still there was no sign that Turkey was cooperating. It was not for lack of trying by others. Senators Lankford, Shaheen, and Tillis had introduced a bill to block the transfer of the F-35 fighter planes, and ninety-eight members of the EU parliament—from twenty-one nations—had signed on to a letter asking Turkey for my release. But now President Trump moved as well, backing up his threat with action.

The US Treasury implemented the Global Magnitsky Act, blocking the assets of Turkey's justice minister and interior minister, two men they accused of being responsible for my arrest and detention. The main effect of this was to give a message that the US was willing to take steps. The market noted it, and the Turkish lira took an immediate hit. "The relationship is now officially in crisis," said one former government official in the *New York Times*. "And the only way out is for Erdogan to do what he hates the most: back down."

The longer my half freedom went on, the harder it became to imagine going back to prison. At Buca I had been focused in like a marathon runner who is worn out but keeps running, refusing to take a break in fear that he will not be able to start up again. But now I was together with Norine, could talk to our kids, see friends, access news—the list of good things was so long. The day I returned to our apartment I had told Norine, "It's okay if I have to go back, if that's what it takes to fulfill God's plans. I'll be okay. I will just be grateful for this day I have with you." But it was getting harder to think this way.

And yet I could not ignore the possibility that I might well be sent back to prison. Ten days had passed and nothing had happened. Relations between the two countries were low and getting lower.

"Norine," I said quietly one morning. "What if they're not letting us go?"

24 | THE BRUNSON CRISIS

I WAS LOCKED IN. The police had buttoned down security so tight on the street that one newspaper reported that "even the birds cannot fly without permission." They checked Norine's purse and even her grocery bags when she came back from the store, and whenever our friends came to visit us they were stopped, searched, and their ID and images sent through to the prosecutor's office before they were allowed in.

We were advised to cut back on visitors and just wait. The media would try to talk to Norine whenever she went to our church, and photographers often lay in wait when she left the relative safety of our cordoned-off street. We kept as low a profile as we possibly could, not talking to anyone in the media—in Turkey or at home. We stayed away from Facebook and wrote no letters to anyone about our case.

The Turkish press became obsessed with my story. Badly photo-shopped images of me appeared in the papers—me on a joker card, me on the dollar bill, my head stuck on Rambo's body. Every story ended by repeating as fact the same old accusations against me. It was very frustrating that no matter what answers Cem or I gave in court, or how thoroughly we discredited the witnesses, the media never reported any of it.

It did not take long for the media to get even more intense. They had good reason to. When it became clear that President Erdogan was not going to be moved by the Magnitsky Act sanctions placed on two of his leading ministers, President Trump doubled the tariffs on Turkish steel and aluminum.

The Turkish lira dropped dramatically. According to some reports, as much as $40 billion was wiped off the Turkish stock market. Everyone was affected. *The Economist* called me "the world's most expensive prisoner." The Turkish media called it "The Brunson Crisis."

I was still stuck in the apartment. It was wonderful to be out of prison, but soon the bars on our windows—standard issue for most Turkish city homes—made me feel like a bird in a cage. And with every passing day the hostility toward me increased. At first it had been mainly Erdogan's supporters who had a reason to be mad at me, because I was accused of being in league with Fethullah Gulen. Then all the people who despised the PKK turned on me when the media started that line. But now, with inflation rising and the markets tanking, everybody in the country had reason to hate me. Between twenty and thirty police and soldiers were on guard around our little building at all times. There was usually a police or military armored vehicle parked outside. They weren't there to keep me in—they were there to keep others out. I was told not to go out on our balcony or stand in front of windows for fear of snipers. They had made me a target.

There was a whirlwind going on and I was getting the blame. I even read that the contagion was spreading to emerging markets and that Argentina was about to default on its debt because of investors pulling out of Turkey. Yet the Turkish economy had structural problems that had been there for a long time. The sanctions President Trump was imposing were simply the straw that broke the camel's back, as investors spooked and started to pull out of Turkey. But Erdogan seized the opportunity to pin all Turkey's financial problems on the US, and on me.

The death of the Turkish economy appeared to be just around the corner, and President Trump announced that he was prepared to do more than just hike the tariffs. On one call back home with a friend who was working closely with the White House, we heard Trump's plan boiled down to its most simple, powerful form: "He knows that there's a price they're willing to pay, and a price they're not willing to pay."

I THOUGHT A LOT ABOUT PHARAOH in those days. I wondered whether something similar was going on with Erdogan. In the Bible, Moses was calling for Pharaoh to let his people go, but Pharaoh kept hardening his heart. Was Erdogan's heart being hardened? Why else would he allow Turkey to be so badly affected? Several times in the last couple of years the Turkish government had made moves toward resolving my case, and then pulled back. Would they do the same thing again? Because instead of trying to repair relations with the US, Erdogan seemed to be raising the stakes.

And President Trump was not backing down. On August 17, he tweeted: "Turkey has taken advantage of the United States for many years. They are now holding our wonderful Christian Pastor, who I must now ask to represent our Country as a great patriot hostage. We will pay nothing for the release of an innocent man, but we are cutting back on Turkey!" We weren't sure what the implications were of being asked to be a "patriot hostage." Jay Sekulow, who was also one of Trump's lawyers now, called us to explain: Wait. Be patient for this to be done the right way.

The media reports grew darker and darker. They were no longer just content with running polls about sending me back to prison, they were openly speculating on the plots to kill me. Some suggested that the CIA had me listed as a target ("The same way they knocked down their own towers on 9/11"), while others argued that Israeli Mossad would be more likely to kill me as it would have the added benefit of messing up the relationship between the US and Turkey. Still others said that there were CIA and Mossad teams staying in apartments near our house, but their goal was to rescue, not to kill me. To some these were just harmless conspiracy theories, but I knew that the media in Turkey was no more independent than the judiciary. They could be preparing the ground for some scenario, just in case. Maybe some disaffected group—a faction within the government, or powerful businessmen—would take action to remove the problem and put an end to the crisis. I could be killed. Or disappear. Or be spirited out of Turkey and set loose. This could be done independently, or even with Erdogan's secret approval. I didn't sit around worrying about it, but I considered the possibilities. In Turkey, a land of intrigue and conspiracies, anything could happen.

Once or twice a week I would jump from bed in the middle of the night, jerked from sleep by pounding on our door and the insistent ringing of the doorbell. The police were conducting random checks to make sure I was still in the apartment. Whether night or day, I never knew what would happen. I could be taken to prison at a moment's notice, or just taken. When I answered the door I did it with cell phone in hand, a text message ready to send in case it were needed.

Soon after I was released to house arrest I had tried to come off my medication, cutting out the sleeping meds and antidepressants and dropping down the Xanax. But as the tension mounted and the prospect of going back to prison grew, my anxiety rose. I did not want to be on meds, but it wasn't hard to see that I needed to go back to my original Xanax dose.

And I also needed to listen to my wife. Several times in the afternoon Norine came home and found me bouncing around, anxious and disturbed.

"What have you been reading?"

I'd show her a video of protestors smashing Apple products on the street or burning dollars while they were shouting "Allahu Akbar," or I'd point out an article in which Erdogan talked of economic war and said, "You dare to sacrifice 81 million Turks for a priest who is linked to terror groups?" I thought it was the other way around, that Erdogan was willing to push his relationship with the US to the breaking point just to keep me in prison. And my fear was that at some point President Trump could decide the price was too high—even though I was an innocent man. The miracle was that Trump was not backing down.

Norine would tell me to stop reading and watching anything about me. I knew she was right.

IT WASN'T JUST THE MEDIA that fueled my apprehensions. Norine was out at church one afternoon in September. I was midway through a workout on a treadmill, covered in sweat and out of breath, when the police called up.

"There's a priest here to see you. Father James?"

I thought I recognized the name as someone from an Anglican church in Izmir, so I told them to let him up.

When I opened the door I realized that I was mistaken. Father James wasn't who I thought he was, and he wasn't alone either. He introduced me to the two men he was with, an American businessman and a Turkish lawyer. I decided to hear them out.

"A lot of Turkish companies have foreign debt," said the businessman. "Some are going to be forced to close soon, and there are a lot of business leaders in Turkey and the US that want this resolved."

I was wary. Was this the kind of situation we had been concerned about, where a group might try to get me out without Erdogan's knowledge and make things even worse for me in the process? I told them that whatever they had to say I wanted Norine to hear as well, so I gave her a quick call.

"You need to come home right now. I'm not in trouble but there are some people here."

She was back within a few minutes, ready to hear the businessman continue with his story.

"We've just flown from the US by private jet and we're meeting with President Erdogan tomorrow. We're private, and represent relationships between businessmen in the US and businessmen in Turkey. We all want to see this resolved and expect that it will be tomorrow and when it is we'd like to take you home. So, be ready. You can bring a bag or two with you."

Neither of us knew what to say. He showed us some pictures on his phone of him with various high-profile people in the US government, and after a few more words, they left.

Norine went to look from the window. "What do you think?" I said. "If they were trying to keep this a secret it didn't work. Look."

The three of them had made it past the police cordon out on the street and walked into a media ambush. Father James in his flowing Franciscan robe attracted most of the attention, but he walked through the reporters with the most beautiful, winsome smile and did not say a word. When they'd finally battled through the crowd and made it into an SUV with government plates, Norine voiced the question I was asking myself. "So, do we pack?"

"I guess."

BY THE TIME THE FOURTH TRIAL DATE was just days away, nothing had changed. The businessmen had not been able to persuade Erdogan, so we hadn't gotten on that private jet. Even though I'd promised Norine that I would stay away from news sites, with the trial so close I found it hard to resist. Although the Turkish economy was battered, Erdogan was still refusing to back down. In an address to Turkey's parliament he had accused me of having "dark ties to terror groups," and other government officials were openly advocating for my return to prison. The speculation in the media was split. Some were convinced that I was about to be released, while others were adamant that I would soon be back behind bars serving my thirty-five years.

Many sleepless nights I lay in bed and prayed, "I desperately want to return to my children. But if you are not yet finished with what you want to accomplish by my being imprisoned, or by my being sent back to prison, then give me strength, courage, and endurance to be faithful to the end. I am afraid. Oh God, let me go, but if not, help me to be faithful."

I did not know what would happen. Nobody did. Maybe Erdogan himself did not yet know what he was going to do. But I determined what I would say if they sent me back to prison: "You can defeat me— that is not so difficult to do. But you cannot defeat the Jesus who lives in me."

THE DAY BEFORE THE HEARING, the chargé d'affaires to Turkey visited, along with Tony Perkins, president of the Family Research Council but acting in his capacity as a USCIRF commissioner. Tony had met with President Trump the day before, and handed us a letter.

> *Dear Pastor Andrew*
> *We are praying for you, and we are working to bring you home.*
> *Keep the faith. We will win!*
> *God bless you.*
>
> > *Sincerely*
> > *Donald Trump*

It was a touching gesture, and we both appreciated it greatly.
But that night I still packed two bags.
One to go back to the States.
One to go back to prison.

25 | THIRTY-NINE HOURS

MY ALARM RANG AT 4:30 A.M. on the day of the trial, but I was awake already. All night I'd been thinking, praying, trying to imagine what the day would bring. Would I end up in prison? Was this my last night of freedom? Or would it be my last night in Turkey? So many different possibilities had flooded my mind, and I had no idea what to expect.

Others seemed more certain, but their opinions were divided. There was plenty of discussion about how best to get me out of the country in the event I was released. I could remain in police custody and be deported from Istanbul, or even accompanied all the way to the US by Turkish police. Or, they could release me to the embassy, but there were no quick options as there would be no flights available until the next day. Cem, on the other hand, had been trying to convince me that there was no way the case would be wrapped up by the end of the day. "They're not going to find you guilty right away and they won't put you back in prison right away either. The sequence of things does not work that way. They present their evidence, you present yours. We're still a long ways off."

Even so, when the police came for me at 5:15 a.m., the one bag I picked up was the bag I had packed for prison.

One of the officers paused and looked at it. "What's in it?"

"My Bible, some clothes. Things I'll need for prison."

He shook his head. "You can't take that—just your court papers."

I was unhappy, but before I could say anything Norine quietly reassured me, "It's okay, my love, I'll get it to you somehow if you need it."

THE MORNING SESSION began with the recall of one of the prosecutor's main witnesses against us. Levent had been a member of our church, and on the third trial day he had accused me of hiding FETO fugitives in our house of prayer after the coup and of working with a Kurdish bomb maker—information that he said he had been told by two different people. Cem had protested and now the prosecutor had brought in both witnesses who he said would back up Levent's claims.

I recognized both of them. The first witness lived next door to the house of prayer, and when it came time for the prosecutor to ask him to confirm that he had been the one who told Levent about my support of the FETO members, the man shook his head. "No," he said. "I never told him that. He's the one who told me."

I was amazed. But there was more to come.

When the prosecutor asked the second witness whether he was the source of the information about my being friends with a Kurdish bomb maker, he denied it completely. "Levent is the one who told me. I don't know anything about it—I'm just a simple cook minding my own business."

I was happy that Levent was being exposed as a liar. But there was still more to come.

The jumbotron screens flickered and another witness appeared. After he was sworn in and was asked a question, he laid out the truth. "No, you've got it wrong. This is what really happened . . ." He completely undermined one of the main secret witnesses.

I tried to get a read on any of the three judges but they were looking just as stone-faced as ever. The prosecutor, however, was looking disconcerted. He told the court that he was abandoning his final two witnesses—one of whom had accused me of running boatloads of cash to Israel to be channeled to the PKK. The judge announced we were taking an early break for lunch.

I sat alone, too nervous to eat.

ONCE WE RESUMED, things turned bad for me almost immediately. The prosecutor asked for permission to speak, and leaned dramatically into his microphone. "I demand that Andrew Brunson be returned to prison right now for the remainder of his trial."

I looked over at Cem. He looked as surprised as I felt. I had known being sent back to prison was an option, but this was so sudden, and I had hoped they were going to look for a face-saving way to let me go. Things were going in a very bad direction now. In spite of all the threats, all the damage to the Turkish economy, all the chaos this case had unleashed, could it be that they would still hold on to me?

After consulting with his two colleagues, the main judge denied the prosecutor's request.

"Well, in that case," said the prosecutor, "I am ready to make a recommendation to the court and ask for sentencing."

I turned to Cem. He wasn't just surprised anymore, he looked resigned to the fact that the court was going to do what it was going to do. I felt sick with dread. The bile was building in my throat. The prosecutor was resting his case and pushing the judges to rule. It felt like the mouth of hell was opening all over again.

The prosecutor had pulled out a thick document and was reading it out loud to the court—it must have been prepared before the day's session. He was talking so fast that I found it difficult to keep up with him. The clerk gave me a copy and handed one to Cem, and we both started reading, trying to figure out where the prosecutor was heading. Finally I tuned out from his droning and skipped to the last page.

His statement listed all the reasons why he considered me guilty. There were summaries of all the witnesses who had appeared at the previous trials, including those whom Cem had discredited and even the ones who had just been discredited that very morning. It was as if all our objections, responses, and explanations had fallen on deaf ears. Worse, he was demanding that I be convicted. Any hope that I'd experienced earlier on vanished. Pharaoh had hardened his heart again.

235

I glanced at Cem. He wasn't listening to the prosecutor either. He had pulled out a reference book and was looking up the specific penal codes listed on the last page and the sentencing guidelines, adding up the years.

It took almost thirty minutes for the prosecutor to read through his statement in full, and when he finished the court was silent. I wanted to shout out that this wasn't how things were supposed to be done, but I just sat there, stunned.

The judge started his own summing up, announcing that the court would not hear any of my witnesses nor accept any of the material we wanted to submit as exculpating evidence.

My heart was numb. A single thought echoed in my mind: *They're going to convict me*. I was sure that I was going to prison again. The only question was for how long.

"Do you want to make a final defense?"

I looked back at the judge. Present a defense? How could I present a defense? We had our own witnesses who were eager to testify. In addition to the audio and video clips, there were affidavits, text messages, and emails that would help expose the lies that the prosecutor had spread about me. But the judge was not allowing any of it. Since I'd been under house arrest I'd been able to work so much more effectively on my defense, and had prepared answers to all the false witnesses from the previous sessions. But what would be the point? None of it mattered now. The judge clearly was not interested. It was as good as over.

The judge was losing patience with me. "I said, do you wish to make a final defense?"

I looked over at Cem and back toward Norine. "Your Honor, I'd like to have some time to talk with my lawyer and also with my wife."

"Very well," he said. "You've got ten minutes."

"NORINE," I SAID, my voice choking up, "they want to send me back to prison. They are going to convict me. I know it."

"Wait," said Cem, still flicking through his court handbook. "Look, they've lowered the charges and the things he's asking for carry a sentence of up to fifteen years."

"Fifteen years? I'll be sixty-five. I can't do that! Cem, you hear me?"

"I do, but we cannot really present a defense here. And I don't think they want us to make a defense either. I think something is happening, some decision has been taken already. Let me go back and talk to the judge."

Cem left Norine and me standing on either side of the low barrier that separated me from the rest of the court. I remembered what Sam Brownback had said to Norine—that the case against me wouldn't last five minutes in a US court.

I couldn't read Cem's face when he returned, but his voice sounded calm. "The judge says that the prosecutor is calling for a mild sentence and that they would lower it for good behavior and your demeanor in court. I don't know what they're going to give you, but it's clear they've made a decision already. There's no point in prolonging this as they aren't going to accept anything we say. They don't want you to make a defense, so I say let's not present one. Just say a few sentences. I'll make a couple of points and we'll just see what they do."

I opened my mouth but no words came. I could just nod my head. Norine hugged me. I returned to my seat and started writing as the judges began to file in. I had so little time, but if I was going to say something before they sentenced me, what should I say?

All too soon the judge started to speak. "We're ready to proceed," he announced. "What is your defense?"

My legs felt weak as I stepped out to the microphone in front of the dais. The judges seemed to tower above me even higher than usual. My mouth was dry. I could hear no sound from the scores of people sitting in the back behind me.

"I am an innocent man," I said, glad that my voice was sounding a lot calmer than I feared it would. "I love Jesus. I love Turkey."

237

The judge didn't react, but turned to Cem. After listening to a few further comments from him, the three judges stood up and left the dais to decide my fate.

I stayed seated and picked up my pen again. I wanted to write down what I was thinking, to capture this moment and be ready to say something when the final verdict came. I felt so desperate, so alone, so shattered. After wondering if I was on the brink of being set free, after my government had taken unprecedented steps to secure my release, I was about to be convicted and sent to prison. For life? It might as well be. In fifteen years my kids would be grown up, there would be grandchildren I'd never held. And my wife—how difficult this would be for her. How could I possibly survive so long in such terrible isolation?

"I am innocent," I wrote. "I am a missionary. I'm a prisoner for the sake of Jesus. Please do not forget me, my wife, my children. I ask Christians, pray for me. This is a weight I do not know how to bear. May Jesus give me the courage to endure to the end. I love Turkey. I love Jesus."

I put the pen down. There was nothing else to write.

I turned and looked for Norine. They had allowed me to talk with her before, so I motioned her over. We leaned into each other over the barrier, forehead to forehead. Norine prayed, "Lord, we really need you here. We need you here now. We are calling on your name."

When she was done I whispered my fear. "Norine, they're going to send me to prison. They're going to send me to prison."

"Wait, my love. Just wait. Cem says something is going on here."

"No. They're sending me to prison, Norine. That's what is happening."

I heard movement at the front of the court and knew the judges were back. I didn't want to let go of my wife. I didn't know when I would be able to hold her like this again.

I STOOD when the judge told me to stand and listened to him deliver his verdict. "This court finds you guilty, of willingly and knowingly supporting a terrorist group, without being a member. You are sentenced to five years . . ."

His words blurred. My head was spinning. He was still talking, saying something about the political nature of the crime and how that affected my sentencing, but all I heard was "guilty" and "five years."

I looked down at the piece of paper I'd been writing on. It was still true: I was still innocent, even though they'd found me guilty. And I still loved Jesus.

The judge was still talking.

I wondered what would happen next. *Would they send me back to Buca? Would I be able to have my old cell back with Nejat?*

There was silence in the court.

I looked up to see the judge staring at me.

"Well," he said, waving his hand at me. "That's it."

I didn't understand. Was I supposed to go over and find the military police who were going to take me back to prison? I looked over at Cem. He was walking toward me, smiling. "You're free," he said.

"What?"

"They lowered it to three years, one month, fifteen days, then took off the time served. The prosecutor removed his demands to send you to prison and so you're released pending appeal."

"So, what, I'm under house arrest?"

"No. Your travel ban has been lifted. You're free. You can go home. To the US."

While Cem went to tell Norine I turned to the judges and thanked them. I even thanked the prosecutor. Then Norine was running toward me and we knelt down on the floor. "Thank you, God," we prayed. "Thank you. Thank you. Thank you, God."

I WAS TAKEN BACK to Izmir in a police car that was following a military armored vehicle. It was like the parting of the Red Sea. I tried not to think about Pharaoh chasing the Israelites once he'd agreed to let them go.

While Norine and the others battled through the Friday rush-hour traffic, I waited in the apartment with the handful of police officers who had accompanied me. They removed the ankle bracelet, took down the transmitter and gave me some forms to sign. While doing this I received a call from the US consul to tell me a plane was on its way from Germany. I was very relieved to hear this, and grateful to President Trump. Apparently Tony Perkins had gotten in touch with the White House the day before and communicated that if I were released speed would be critical in getting us out of the country.

One of the officers walked over to me. "There's another call for you," he said. "The chief prosecutor of Izmir."

My head spun. I remembered the wolf. The man who glared at me in Karakaya's office in Izmir with nothing but hatred in his eyes. "Okan Batu?"

The officer shook his head. Okan Batu was no longer chief prosecutor, and his replacement had been appointed by Ankara. He handed me the phone. I knew that any prosecutor had the power to protest any decision the court made. If they wanted me back in prison, they could send me there instantly. So the embassy's first priority was to get me out of the country as soon as possible before anything—a tweet, a statement by a government official, a dumb comment from me—might give the Turkish government reason to send me back. Until I left Turkish airspace I would not be safe.

The prosecutor was direct. "Do you have plans to leave?"

"Yes. Right now the embassy is making plans. There's a plane coming from Germany to take us away."

"How long will it take?"

"I—I don't know. It's on the way and should be here very soon. They're planning on us leaving tonight."

I looked up. One of the embassy staff had arrived, and I handed him the phone. I did not want to talk to the prosecutor for one second longer than I had to.

I SPENT A COUPLE OF HOURS with our closest friends who had come to say goodbye while Norine packed some of her things. It was strange leaving like this, for things to be so rushed after more than two years of waiting. But we were eager to get out of the country. We had to get away from the apartment, away from the crowds and the media, and from the risk that something could so easily go wrong.

The chargé d'affaires drove us to the airport in his armored SUV. I was aware of the chaos all around us, but it was like it was happening to someone else. The crush as we pushed our way through the media to the private terminal at the airport, the calm as we had our passports checked inside, even the moment we walked up the steps and pulled down the blinds inside the Air Force plane, it was all happening to someone else, not me.

I watched the map as we took off, willing the pilot to head west out to sea and into Greek airspace. But we hugged the Turkish coast heading northwest. When the captain finally announced that we had left Turkish airspace, all I could think was that the nightmare was finally over.

It was 1:30 a.m. when we arrived at the US base at Ramstein. We could not believe that the ambassador to Germany was waiting in the cold air to greet us, holding a folded US flag. "Welcome home," he said, handing me the flag. I buried my face in it and wholeheartedly said, "I love my country."

AS WE LANDED at Andrews Air Force Base later that day, I could see our children lined up on the tarmac. We had requested that there be no media so we could freely focus on them, hug, and cry.

And then, just one day after I'd walked out of court, we were driven to the White House. Our kids were taken off to wait while Norine and I were escorted to the Map Room.

WITHIN MINUTES President Trump walked in. He was taller than I imagined, an imposing figure, but with a smile so big and so genuine. "It's good to have you here," he said, shaking my hand. "Do you want a Tic Tac?"

That threw me. I was going to say no, but how often does the president offer you a Tic Tac? "Sure!" I said, holding out my hand and watching three of them drop onto my palm. I threw two in my mouth and slipped the last in my pocket. We thanked him and talked for a few minutes, then we all walked outside, down the colonnade, and into the Oval Office.

It was the chair that got me. As soon as I walked in the room, I recognized it—the chair that President Erdogan had sat in when he had visited the US for the summit. The chair he'd sat in when I'd been watching from my prison cell. The chair he'd sat in and let his heart be hardened as my president asked for my release. Erdogan kept me in prison for seventeen more months after he'd sat there.

It was the same chair that President Trump motioned for me to sit in.

Just the day before, the judge had declared me guilty of terrorism. Now I was sitting in the Oval Office next to the president of the United States. On one side sat my reunited family. On the other were Secretary Pompeo, Senator Tillis, Senator Lankford, and others who had worked so diligently to free me. But behind them, unseen, were hundreds of thousands of people across the world who had carried me out on a huge wave of prayer.

After several minutes, I spoke up. There was something Norine and I wanted to do, and we were ready.

"Mr. President, we would like to pray for you. We pray for you often as a family. My wife and I pray for you."

"Well, I probably need it more than anybody in this room so that would be very nice, thank you."

"Can we pray for you now?"

"Yes. Thank you very much."

As I knelt down beside him, he bowed his head. The room went still.

"Lord God, I ask that you pour out your Holy Spirit on President Trump, that you give him supernatural wisdom to accomplish all the plans you have for this country . . ."

EPILOGUE

LESS THAN TWO MONTHS AFTER MY RELEASE, the UN Working Group on Arbitrary Detention concluded that the Turkish authorities targeted and arrested me on the basis of my nationality and faith. They confirmed that I was the victim of religious persecution and declared that the appropriate remedy would be to expunge my criminal record and accord me an enforceable right to compensation and other reparations. They urged the Turkish government to conduct an investigation and take appropriate measures against those who had violated my rights. Finally, they urged the Turkish government to "disseminate the present opinion through all available means and as widely as possible."

So far, the Turkish government has done none of these. The foreign minister still refers to me in public as a spy and calls me Agent Brunson. When a gunman killed fifty people in a mosque in New Zealand in March 2019, Turkish media suggested that I was the one who had given the killer his orders.

This is the new normal in Turkey. The Turkish media—behind which stands the Turkish government—used me to paint a public image of Christians as traitors, terrorists, and enemies of Turkey when nothing could be further from the truth. This deliberate propaganda campaign has led to a rise in hate speech against Christians. We are very proud of the small but brave Turkish church that continues to stand for Jesus in an openly hostile environment.

IN PRISON I often questioned with distress why I struggled so much, especially in comparison to some of my spiritual heroes—or at least what their biographies say about them. I decided that if I ever had the opportunity, I would be open and honest about my struggles, that my testimony would be one of weakness: my weakness, but God's strength. Maybe God chose a weak man to serve as an encouragement to others who feel weak.

I understand persecution, yet I was unprepared for what happened to me. In part this is because I counted the cost for some things, but never for prison—I don't know of any other missionary who has been imprisoned in Turkey. But what really broke me was unmet expectations. I expected that God would intervene to carry me above my circumstances into joy, that even in grief I would feel strength and an infusion of grace, and most importantly, that I would have a sense of his presence. Instead, I felt abandoned by God. The truth is, God's faithfulness and loyalty and love are never put to the test in our difficulties; it was my faithfulness, my loyalty, my love for him that was being tested.

In my case, not sensing his presence was part of the test.

I had to learn the lesson of Isaiah 50:10: "Let him who walks in darkness and has no light trust in the name of the LORD and lean on his God." God was teaching me to stand in the dark, to persevere apart from my feelings, perceptions, and circumstances.

It is clear to me, especially as I remember my weakness and brokenness, that God's grace brought me through. Mostly it was an unfelt grace, but it was there. I had a part as well: I had to cooperate with God. At every point, every time I was broken, I had a choice to make, and I chose to turn my face toward God. I had doubts, questions, I complained and fought with God, but eventually I would once again embrace him. I never stopped talking to him:

No matter what you do or don't do, I will follow you.

I want to keep my face turned toward you, Jesus, like the sunflower that follows the sun throughout the day.

I don't need an answer to my questions to have a relationship with you, God.

As I look back on my prison time—and I am still processing it—I see a pattern. I would get hit with a test, break and go low, and then work slowly toward a point of surrender to God, only to face a harder blow and go even lower. But each time, I started to climb again and eventually made it back to surrender—a deeper surrender, because now I was more aware of the price. There were many ups and downs, but there was a gradual upward trajectory. This was a choice.

I am glad to have escaped the valley of the wolves. And yet there is something I miss from that terrible ordeal. A dear friend told me of a conversation he had with Richard Wurmbrand. In spite of the miserable conditions and torture he endured, there were times when he wished to be back in his solitary prison cell where he had tasted an unusual intimacy with God. I understand him in some small degree, for the conditions of imprisonment—the isolation, threats, and fears—drove me to cling to God as never before. They also brought a rare clarity about what really matters. My every day in prison became consumed with seeking God, drawing close to him. Now I am free, and so grateful for my freedom. But I miss being so completely dependent on God and want to recapture the desperate seeking I had then.

MOST OF THIS BOOK has been a story about one man in a cell. But in truth there was something much bigger going on: God's story.

From the beginning—before the beginning—God was setting things up, like the ultimate Grandmaster chess player. Can it be a coincidence that Philip Kosnett, the chargé d'affaires at the embassy in Ankara during most of my imprisonment, happens to be a member of our home church in a small town in North Carolina? Or that Secretary of State Mike Pompeo is a member of my denomination? And that Vice President

Mike Pence was attending one of its churches, where the pastor prayed every Sunday for my release? Or that Jay Sekulow, who as head of the ACLJ had taken on my case, then became one of President Trump's attorneys? Yes, I had become a pawn, but the Grandmaster was on my side.

It may be a miracle that I was released, but I think it was an even greater miracle that so much was done to release me. I am still amazed at the unprecedented steps that my government took. It was the first time they imposed trade sanctions or used the Magnitsky Act on a NATO ally. The policy on Syria was affected. Congressmen and congresswomen, two thirds of the Senate, European parliamentarians—they all advocated on my behalf. There were other countries involved as well—Mauritania, Sudan, Hungary, Israel, Monaco, Canada, the UK—all asking for the release of a Christian pastor whom nobody had ever heard of.

All of this was necessary, because it took unprecedented steps to pry me out of Turkey. There was no guarantee that I would be freed. We learned that even on the night before the last day of trial, with the Turkish economy battered and the threat of more sanctions if my case were not resolved, the Turkish government demanded that the US pay $1.9 billion for my release. They were turned down flat.

I believe so many intervened on my behalf because all over the world Christians were praying for me as I was held hostage. Some have said I was the most prayed for man in the world. I don't know if this was the case, and certainly while in prison I did not have the wider view of what was going on; although Norine told me, I was too overwhelmed by my circumstances to take it in. But even as the chants filled my cell at Sakran, so too, the church of Jesus Christ raised a powerful voice to heaven that would change everything, starting with my heart. Night and day, God's people cried out their distress in prayer, even when I could not. I continue to be astounded that so many prayed for so long and with such intensity.

Why? Most prisoners do not receive this kind of attention; many are unknown except in heaven.

One of the main reasons is that now there are millions of people who have prayed for Turkey, who have that country on their radar. This was God's plan all along. My assignment had been to help prepare for a spiritual harvest. Prison did not cut short my assignment, it served it in the most effective way. God used my imprisonment to orchestrate an unprecedented worldwide prayer movement. I rode a wave of prayer out of Turkey. But a tsunami of prayer from God's people has crashed into Turkey, and this is going to bring great blessing to its people.

A Turkish believer said, "The whole world is praying for us with a single voice—imagine what we can do with all that prayer."

That God had a master plan also provides the best explanation for why things went so completely wrong on the two dates I thought God had set for freeing me. It is only with hindsight, access to my journals, and comparing notes with Norine, that I have begun to understand what happened. After returning to the States I was startled to read in my Harmandali journal that just a few days before I was sent to Sakran Prison the thought kept going through my mind: *Are you willing to stay if it will bring greater glory?* And I said, *Yes.* So, on December 12, 2016, instead of being set free a court confirmed I should be kept in prison.

As for May 22, 2017, the two governments did in fact reach an agreement on this date I had received in a dream sixty-eight days earlier. But the next day—when she was supposed to be getting ready to go— Norine woke up with a song playing in her mind: "I Surrender All." And so she did. The day after this Turkey pulled out of the agreement. Something like this happened several other times. We think it is possible that God would have shortened the imprisonment, but because we were willing to surrender—although without knowing what we were surrendering to—he extended it in order to raise up this movement of prayer. It is as if God were saying, "I can take you out now, but if you stay I will do a greater work." Now I realize what a privilege God gave me.

Norine told me a number of times, "If we are faithful with this, and go through in the right way, we will say we have no regrets because of what it will accomplish."

We have no regrets.

I WAS ERDOGAN'S HOSTAGE, but only until God accomplished what he intended to through my imprisonment.

And then, at the right time, God kept his word—the word he gave to me right before all of this started, the word I clung to throughout my imprisonment. *It's time to come home.*

He brought me home.

Worthy of My All

You are worthy, worthy of my all
My tears and pain I lift up as an offering
Teach me to share in the fellowship of your suffering
Lamb of God, you are worthy of my all

You are worthy, worthy of my all
Adopted as a son, a brother to my King
Indeed, I will share in your glory if I share your suffering
Jesus, you are worthy of my all

You are worthy, worthy of my all
But my heart faints, drowned in sorrow, overwhelmed
Make me like you, Cross-bearer, persevering, faithful to the end
To stand the trial and receive the crown of life

You are worthy, worthy of my all
This is my declaration in the darkest hour
Jesus, the Faithful One who loves me, always good and true
You made me yours, you are worthy of my all

I want to be found worthy to stand before you on that day
With no regrets from cowardice, things left undone
To hear you say, "Well done, my faithful friend, now enter your
    reward"
Jesus, my Joy, you are the prize I'm running for

You are worthy, worthy of my all
You are worthy, worthy of my all
What can I give to the Son of God, who gave himself for me
Here I am, you are worthy of my all

Written at Buca Prison, September 10, 2017

NOTES

Andrew Brunson is an American pastor. He holds a PhD in New Testament from the University of Aberdeen, Scotland. Andrew and his wife, Norine, were involved in starting churches, training believers, aiding refugees, and a house of prayer in Turkey for twenty-three years until being falsely accused of terrorism in October 2016. After this, Andrew was held for two years in Turkish prisons. Due to a worldwide prayer movement and significant political pressure from the US government, he was finally sentenced to time served and dramatically released in October 2018.

Download for free:
UnceasingWorship.com/AndrewBrunson

Also Available on:

Authentic

We trust you enjoyed reading this book
from Authentic. If you want to be
informed of any new titles from this author
and other releases you can sign up to the
Authentic newsletter by scanning below:

Online:
authenticmedia.co.uk

Follow us: